LAMENTATIONS
of the
FLAME PRINCESS
ADVENTURES

ADVENTURE ANTHOLOGY: DEATH

CONTENTS

Writing by James Edward Raggi IV

Cover art by Yannick Bouchard   Design and Layout by Jez Gordon

LFP0057

Printed in Finland by Otava Book Printing Ltd.
ISBN, Print: 978-952-7238-22-6   ISBN, PDF: 978-952-7238-23-3

www.lotfp.com

FOREWORD

So for the first time in mass distribution, we present in this 90 page tome the most brutal adventures and supplements ever released for ***Lamentations of the Flame Princess***, a game already known for its brutal adventures. If you're not already familiar with these adventures, you're in for a real rough time. If you're a Referee looking for material for your campaign, you're going to wonder how you could ever present this stuff to real life people without them thinking that you're some sort of truly disturbed person.

But that's kind of the point. Let me explain.

There are two things happening in these adventures. The first is a more surface level, superficial affectation. I like heavy metal. I like horror movies and books. My tastes are a bit weird, but these days not so transgressive in these fields. But it used to be. The most brutal, the most rejective of society and any sort of norms, those artists that sought to overwhelm and traumatize the senses, that's what I used to be all about. Bands like Anal Cunt, songs like Cannibal Corpse's *Necropedophile*, movies like *I Spit On Your Grave* and *Cannibal Holocaust*. Books don't seem to have quite the same effect, probably because even when the text is just the worst, it's not images, and their covers aren't designed to provoke the way album covers are.

But it felt that ***Lamentations of the Flame Princess*** would be a lie if we didn't dabble in this sort of thing every so often. Of the adventures presented in this anthology, the ***Fuck For Satan*** adventure included here is run-of-the-mill, not even noticeable in the world of heavy metal (with a large part of that scene completely removed from corporate distribution and the specialty shops completely used to the attitude and imagery). In comparison, ***Death Love Doom*** certainly hits every disturbing note, but even that isn't as nasty as many metal albums' artwork and themes. Originally, I had intended for realistic artwork to be used for the interior illustrations, but had trouble finding someone willing to do it. One frequent collaborator even claimed what I was trying to commission was illegal and soon after stopped working with me altogether. So we had to go with a more stylized presentation. Even so, I was afraid that releasing the book, even in a limited edition, direct-sales-only format, would result in wider boycotts and banning of ***Lamentations of the Flame Princess*** material. Didn't happen, although I guess with the wider distribution opportunities this present edition will receive, there's still time for that.

People who haven't been exposed to these things before, or people who actively shut out negative thoughts and feelings, are often shocked. But to some of us, acknowledging these sorts of things, thinking about them, exploring them, and yes, even playing with them, are completely normal, everyday things.

The other point of the adventures contained in this anthology is to expose the dark underbelly of the commonplace feel-good fantasy adventure game. The vast majority of the market seeks to represent PG-13 (to use US movie ratings as an analogy) action movie excitement. Violent people doing violent things to other violent people… and it's supposed to feel good.

Let me get this straight.

Player characters are supposed to be heavily armed, landless wanderers, who go into lawless places, often underground, to violently confront supernatural threats as well as other heavily armed people… feeling entitled to take whatever they find and grab as much cash as they can, regardless of any other goals. And the default is to think of them as the good guys, champions of justice punishing the evil.

Mmmhmm.

Now this isn't a criticism of that approach. It's fiction, and fiction helps people enjoy themselves, and never has to be justified. But there other approaches. Like, what would a world be like if there were supernatural creatures and people who harness the ability to break the laws of physics, and landless armed bands coming into violent conflict with each other over power and profit. It would be ugly. Just the worst world possible. And the nature of the creatures, of the supernatural focus, would not be PG-13.

It is my contention that all fantasy would actually be horror if it was real. The entire point of ***Lamentations of the Flame Princess*** is exploring that idea. But this adventure collection? This is the "What if…?" of fantasy taken to its most unflinching, pessimistic, destructive end.

It is probably a bit much to suggest that you enjoy what follows, but I do very much hope you endure.

James Edward Raggi IV
March 20, 2019
Helsinki, Finland

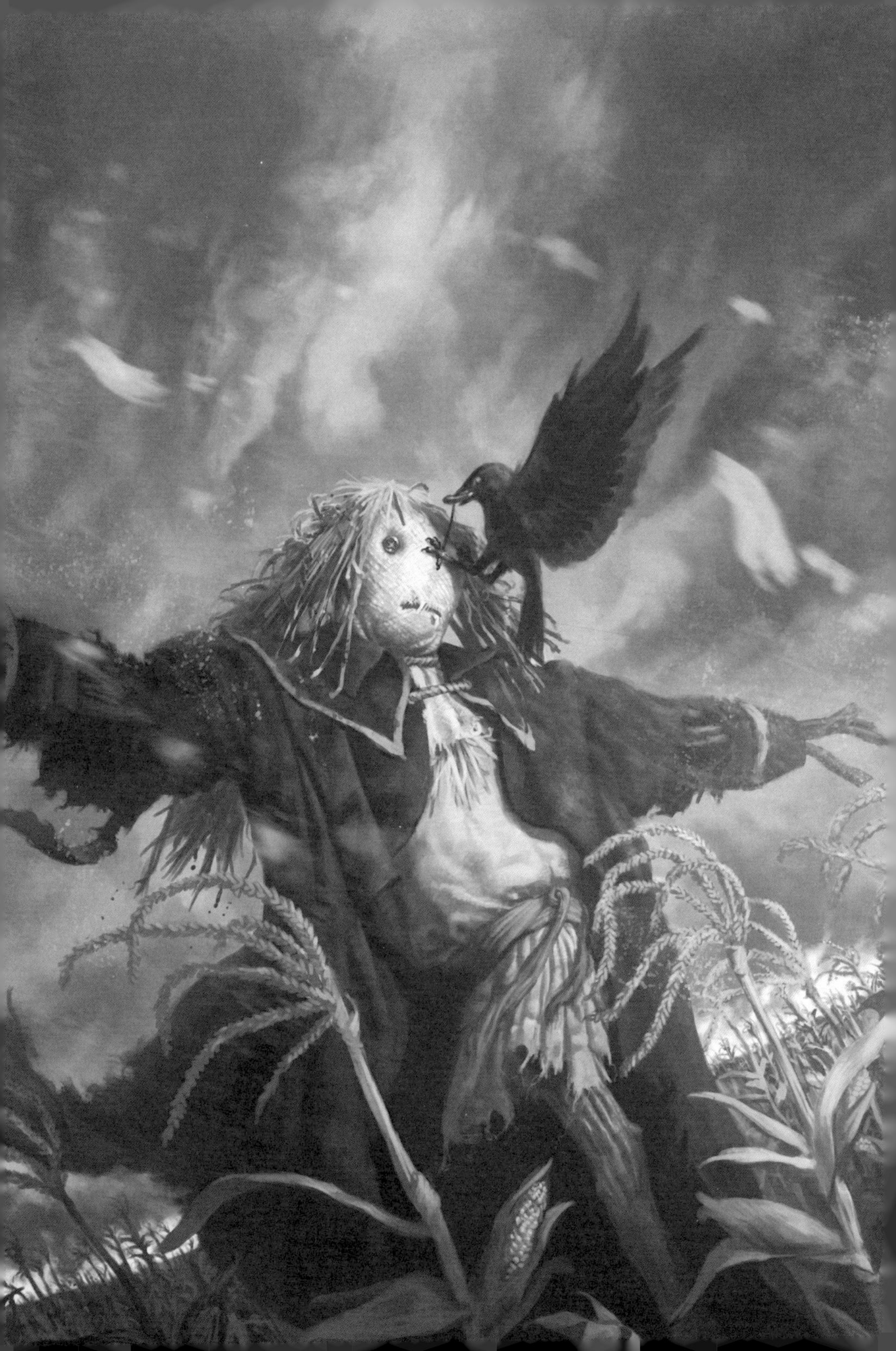

LAMENTATIONS
of the
FLAME PRINCESS
ADVENTURES

TALES OF THE SCARECROW

Written by James Edward Raggi IV
Edited by Matthew Pook
Cover Art by Jason Rainville
Illustration, Cartography and Graphic Design by Jez Gordon
First Printed in 2012

CONTENTS

SETUP

This adventure location can be placed in any out-of-the-way rural area, located along a scenic route between two larger settlements. Somewhere along the route, just off the road, will be a roughly circular lush green cornfield—even out of season. (Yes, the cover shows something else, but when an artist turns in something that great, you don't correct him.) A trail from the road leads through cornfield, leaving a gap in the crop through which can be seen a farmhouse standing in the middle of the field. This might be enough to get the player characters to investigate, but if not, the Referee knows what will entice his players more than any writer would, and he should use that knowledge.

THE FIELD

Below the cornfield lives a gigantic beast which cannot stand the air above. If conditions are right, it can detect the most minute vibrations in the ground around it, and it will use its million tentacles to attempt to snatch prey from the surface.

The "right conditions" are peculiar. Potential prey must be within range of its tentacles (which can reach to the perimeter of the corn field), but not directly above its brain (which is quite coincidentally the same size as the farmhouse and the cleared area inside the cornfield). It also cannot detect targets moving towards its brain, so moving from the outside of the cornfield to the inside renders a potential target safe from attack. Those standing still in the cornfield, or moving away from the farmhouse while still in the cornfield, are subject to attack by the beast.

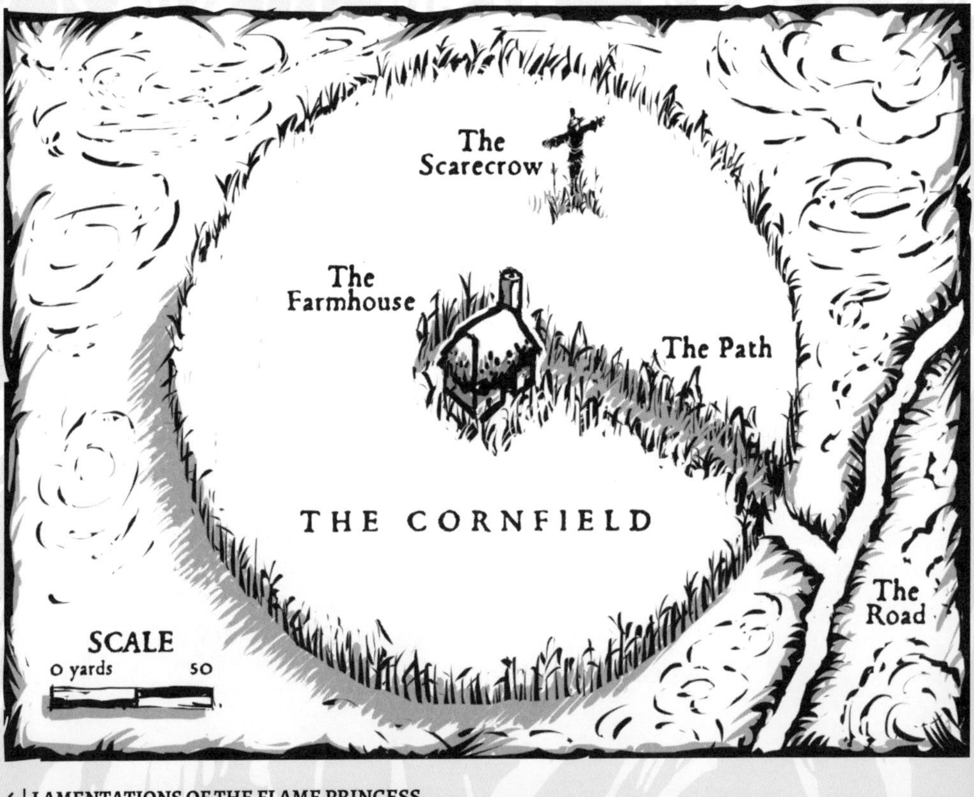

It also finds the open air intolerable, so it can only attack one target with one barbed tentacle each round. It attacks as a 5 Hit Dice monster, doing 1d8 damage per hit. The attack is a fast strike-and-withdraw maneuver, the tentacle's barb tearing away flesh, so unless the victim is acting on the same Initiative number as the monster (or if the character won the Initiative and holds his action until the creature strikes), the tentacle cannot be attacked. Only when a victim falls to the ground and does not move will the creature ignore anything else in the corn field and feed on it, sucking the body through hollows in the tentacle barbs. Note that the tentacles are sufficiently long to attack levitating or flying characters up to 100' off the ground.

Each tentacle is Armor Class 14 with 8 Hit Points. "Killing" a tentacle will cause it to be withdrawn from the surface, but will not deter the creature from continuing to attack with another of its tentacles.

The creature itself is 1000 Hit Dice and except for its tentacles, is immobile.

The corn grows closely together and is a difficult obstacle to move through, reducing movement rates by three-quarters. The corn is poisonous: eating it triggers a save versus Poison in each of the next four turns, with each failure resulting in the consumer suffering 1d8 points of damage.

The corn, thanks to the strange fertilizing influence of the creature below, almost instantly regenerates any damage done to it. Any corn stalks cut down or burned grow back within minutes. The trail from the road to the farmhouse is intentionally kept open as a trap by the creature, and as soon as any victims have entered the clearing around the farmhouse it will allow the corn to grow back in the gap and thus block the easiest route back to the road.

THE SCARECROW

The scarecrow stands at the point in the field indicated on the map. The Creature will not attack anyone within 20' of it, so this area can be used as a safe haven.

However, close examination of the scarecrow itself is not advised: it drains life. If anyone wishes to examine the scarecrow or gets close enough to touch it, confirm with the player first how many Hit Points that his character currently has (whether this involves asking the player or informing him based on your own records depends on the individual style of the Referee). Then begin counting down; this represents actual Hit Point losses for the character until the character is no longer within reach of the scarecrow.

The physical scarecrow itself is mundane. It can be destroyed or burned normally, but its destruction does not cancel or nullify any of the area's effects. The scarecrow is a physical manifestation of the malefic power at work here, but is not its cause.

THE FARMHOUSE

The farmhouse is a small brick structure with wooden flooring and a tiled roof. There are only two features worthy of outside of the house:

- The water pump.
- The horses.

There are several features worthy of note inside of the house:

- The stench of death and rot throughout the house.
- The corpse in the bed in **room B.**
- Another corpse on the floor covered with a blanket in **room C.**
- The live man in **room A**.
- The harpsichord in **room A.**
- The Sword Which is Uncertain, lying on the bed in **room C**.
- Two books, *Malleus Deus* and *Tales of the Scarecrow,* on the table in **room A.**

THE WATER PUMP

The water pump at the side of the house is operational, but the water it draws is thick and foul-smelling. It will quench the thirst of any drinker, but it is full of microscopic parasites— anyone drinking the water will require twice the usual amount of food per day beginning the day after the thick water is first ingested.

After two weeks have passed, the parasites will be visible in the host's urine, at which point the character loses 1d3 points total from his Constitution, Dexterity, and/or Strength (determine randomly). The character must make a saving throw versus Poison. Success means that the character fights off the infection in 2d10 days' time and the ability score points lost are restored. Failure means that the infection and its effects—the increased appetite and the ability point loss—are permanent.

THE HORSES

Four horses lie dead and rotten behind the house, all four still bridled and saddled with saddlebags attached. If the remains are disturbed, evidence of dozens of large puncture wounds on the flank and sides of the horses in contact with the ground will be discovered. The saddlebags are empty except for one which contains a scroll case which holds the receipt of sale for Fox's purchase of the sword and the two books which are detailed below. The seller's name and address is noted on the receipt, and the Referee is encouraged to use this or the additional contents of the saddlebags of his devising to seed campaign-specific information so as to develop further adventure hooks.

THE HARPSICHORD

Despite the dilapidation of the farmhouse, the harpsichord is somehow still in perfect condition. It is finely crafted and worth 10,000sp if it could somehow be removed undamaged from the house. The creature below will not attack while the harpsichord is being played by a skilled musician. If an unskilled character plays the harpsichord, it will enrage the beast below, causing it to make 1d4 attacks per round in the field instead of the usual one attack as long as the playing continues.

THE MEN

The badly decomposed corpse of one man, **Kingsly Addams**, lies on the straw-mattress of the bed in **room B**. Another, that of **Edward Corley,** lies on the floor in **room C** covered with a blanket. A third man, sickly and pale, still lives. His name is **Richard Fox,** and he will barely acknowledge anyone entering the house. He will just sit on the floor in **room A,** staring into space. If disturbed, he will demand food and water, claiming not to have eaten for five days. He will refuse to speak or cooperate in any way until he is given some food and water. Both the body of Edward Corley and Richard Fox himself stink of excrement as they both abandoned hygiene and even rudimentary waste disposal some time ago.

Fox is a wealthy adventurer and collector of odd and bizarre items. On his journey home after collecting his latest crypto-paraphernalia with his three servants, he spotted the farmhouse. He still had some way to go, and expecting to purchase supplies from the residents, he instead decided that they would stay the night once he discovered that the house was abandoned.

The first to die was Nicholas Gristleman, who was unafraid to walk through the corn field after they discovered the path had closed. The others did not see exactly what happened to him, but his screams and the sprays of blood above the corn made it clear that the fields were deadly. The horses refused to enter the fields.

Kingsly Addams was the second to die, after the men's food ran out. He decided to eat some of the corn. He became ill immediately and died within minutes of his companions bringing him inside. Unbeknownst to his fellows, he robbed the man who sold the books and the sword to Fox. Addams attempted to swallow the valuables, but only got a few things down before accidentally biting down on a coin and chipping his tooth. His pouch contains 2gp (both of them with teeth marks) and 47sp, but in his stomach is a small, brilliantly cut ruby worth 1750sp, a platinum charm worth 550sp, and 4gp.

Edward Corley was the last to die, as he and Fox stayed in the house, too afraid to leave despite having quickly gone through their meagre supplies; none of them were expecting to eat on the road at all. Corley eventually starved to death, but Fox, near death himself and quite desperate, resorted to cannibalism. Fox has been picking at Corley's raw flesh the past couple of days, and Corley's left thigh shows the signs of this. It is not enough to sustain Fox, but it staves off death that much longer, although Corley is beginning to get a bit rank. Corley's corpse still wears a gold ring worth 500sp on its left hand, and in a pouch inside Corley's vest, is an exquisite music box worth 1300sp.

If questioned after being fed, Fox will relate the story of what happened to his party (leaving out the cannibalism bit of course). If asked about the sword and books in the room, he will explain that he bought them only recently in [nearest large city], and that he believes that they are quite valuable, but has not had them properly appraised, having bought them quickly because he believed that he was getting such a good deal. If pressed, he will admit to paying 50,000sp total for the three items. He does not know that they are magical. If the player characters offer to help him escape, but only if they are rewarded for doing so, he will reluctantly agree to a 5000sp reward if he is returned home safe, plus 1000sp for each of his companions whose body is returned to his family. (This amount should not count towards experience awards.)

He will not resist if the player characters take the items, but should he return to civilization, Fox will file legal grievances with the appropriate authorities. Note that this will make the authorities aware of the *Malleus Deus,* at least, bringing all of the complications that entails. Fox will soon "disappear."

Despite his weakened state, if Fox discovers that the bodies of his fellows have been looted or robbed, he will attempt to kill the perpetrators and will actively undermine all of their efforts as best he can, even if cooperation with them would be in his best interest.

Richard Fox is a 3rd level Fighter who currently has 2 Hit Points (out of a maximum of 15 Hit Points). He has 12gp and 231sp in a sack ("You should have met me before I bought this junk, I had a cart full of gold!"), a rapier and a dagger, but no other equipment or possessions worthy of note.

THE SWORD WHICH IS UNCERTAIN

This exquisitely decorated rapier (worth 5000sp just for the craftsmanship and inlaid gems and precious metals) is also magical.

It treats all opponents as if it they had Armor Class 14. However, on any attack roll of 16 or 17 (including all modifiers), the sword will instead strike one random nearby target within striking range of the attacker. This target can be friend or foe or indifferent, but it will not be the intended target. When this happens, roll 1d8 for damage twice, and use the higher roll.

If there are no other possible targets when a 16 or 17 is rolled, then the errant strike is "banked," meaning that the next time the sword is used to hit, it will automatically strike an unintended (or perhaps better described as a "target other than the declared target" because players do catch on to these tricks quickly and use them to their advantage, as is proper) target. If this attack roll was 16 or 17, one extra strike is still "banked."

There is no limit to the number of strikes that can be "banked" in this way, but only real attacks intended to cause damage to a target count for the purposes of "banking".

THE SPELLBOOK

One book on the desk is a massive tome called *Malleus Deus*. Any Cleric or Magic-User will recognize the title and although they will not know what is in it until they (try to) read it, they will know that it is supposed to be a book that rends order and understanding from the world.

Religious authorities (of all organized religions, bar none) consider possession of the book a capital crime; even knowing why is grounds for burning if one is not in a "need to know" position.

Clerics will be able to recall stories of people who even jested about possessing a copy found their entire households and even their acquaintances, tortured and killed in order to determine the whereabouts of the book. Magic-Users will have heard stories that the destruction of the Library of Alexandria was a deliberate act committed just to ensure that this one book was destroyed.

Given the book's reputation and the supposed lengths to which the authorities will go to ensure its destruction, surely anyone who values their life would simply let the thing be and leave the area at once, telling no one where they have been or more importantly, that fact that they have seen the book.

As a spellbook, the *Malleus Deus* contains the following number of Magic-User spells:

SPELL LEVEL	SPELLS	SPELL LEVEL	SPELLS
1	2d6	**6**	1d4
2	2d4	**7**	1
3	1d6	**8**	1
4	1d4	**9**	1
5	1d4		

If more than one spell of any particular level is present, then the extra spells of that level are not Magic-User spells, but instead Cleric spells of the same level. These Cleric spells are written in magical script and are Magic-User spells for all intents and purposes, and thus cannot be used by Clerics.

If a Magic-User casts one of these usually-Cleric spells in the presence of a Cleric, that Cleric must make a saving throw versus Magic or never be able to cast that spell again—or at all, if the spell cast is of a higher level than the Cleric can currently cast. This also happens if a Cleric knows such a thing has happened. ("Clever" players of Cleric characters may make a fuss about how their character never picks up on such things, even despite the fact that to a Cleric, such things should be obvious. Fine. The player just declared the character to be both unobservant and oblivious, and a good Referee will remember that.) A Cleric who has lost the use of a spell in this fashion, who relates the events to another Cleric also causes that Cleric to have to save versus Magic or lose use of the spell.

Determine all spells in the book randomly.

TALES OF THE SCARECROW

The other book on the desk is a storybook titled *Tales of the Scarecrow*. It is a creepy horror anthology with all of the stories concerning, you guessed it, evil scarecrows.

What exactly happens in the stories? The players will determine that.

The players should be told that each of them will determine, in secret, the possible powers and effects of the scarecrow. Whoever comes up with the most interesting (and/or dangerous) effects will have their entry become the actual power of the scarecrow, and that player's character will receive an experience bonus.

(If they ask how much of a bonus, tell them the truth—it will be random. There is every possibility it will be a negligible increase, every possibility of many thousands of experience points being awarded, and every possibility of something in between.)

Let them know that they do not have to make the scarecrow a monster or assign abilities or powers to the scarecrow itself; it can merely have an effect on the area inside the cornfield or anyone within it. Nor do the effects have to follow any established game mechanics. Any described effects cannot name a specific character or class (unless every character or class receives an individual effect, in which case it is okay; also, "the first one to do x" is acceptable, but any sort of "Yeah, I'm screwing Josh's character but good with this one!" stuff is not.). *Tales of the Scarecrow* is a book of scary stories and whatever the players invent should work in that context.

Tell them that the entry which leaves the party in the worst position will likely win the experience award, so they need to weigh their desire to get experience against the disadvantages of creating a truly debilitating or horrific effect.

Give each player ten (or fifteen, or whatever you think is appropriate) minutes to invent these effects without discussing his idea with his fellow players—this is not a collaborative exercise. These should be written down and each player must sign his idea so that the Referee can tell which player wrote which entry.

The entries must then be passed to the Referee, who should choose the entry that is the most sinister and diabolical before putting it into effect. The "winning" player's character will then be awarded experience according to the following chart with the player being allowed to make all of the rolls instead of the Referee:

D6	EXPERIENCE INCREASE
1	+1d100 percent
2	+2d20 x 100
3	Total of all ability scores x 1d100
4	Reroll every digit of the character's current experience point total on a d10, and continue until each digit comes up an equal or larger number. For example, if a character currently has 4425xp, re-roll the 4, the 4, the 2, and the 5 each on 1d10 and replace the previous number with the number rolled if it is a higher number. If the number rolled is not equal or greater than the current number, reroll.
5	+ 1d10 x 10 percent
6	+ the character's current level x 750.

While the character gains the experience immediately (and this bonus is not subject to any "only gain one level per session" rules), the character will not actually increase in level until he has returned to a safe area.

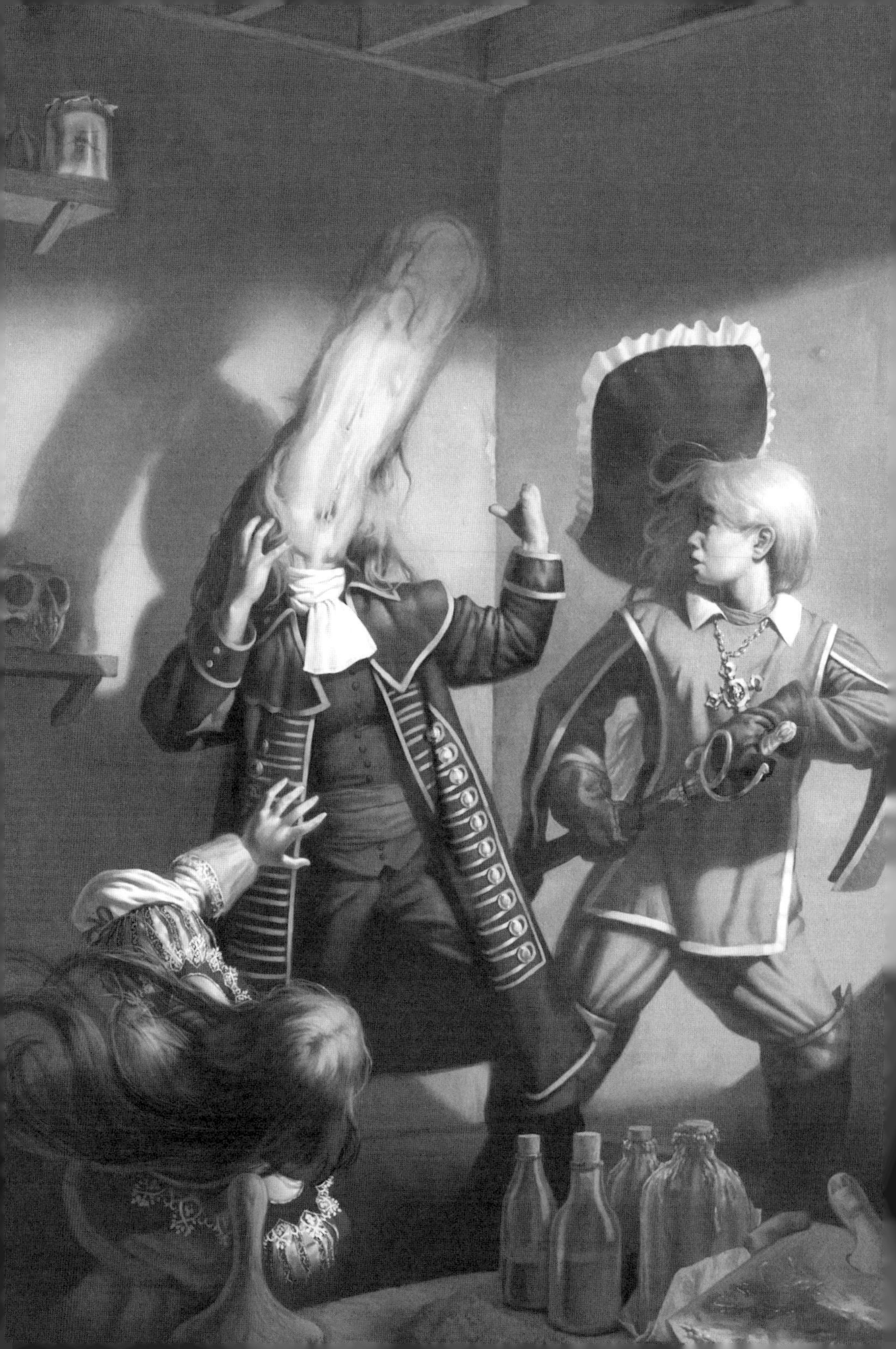

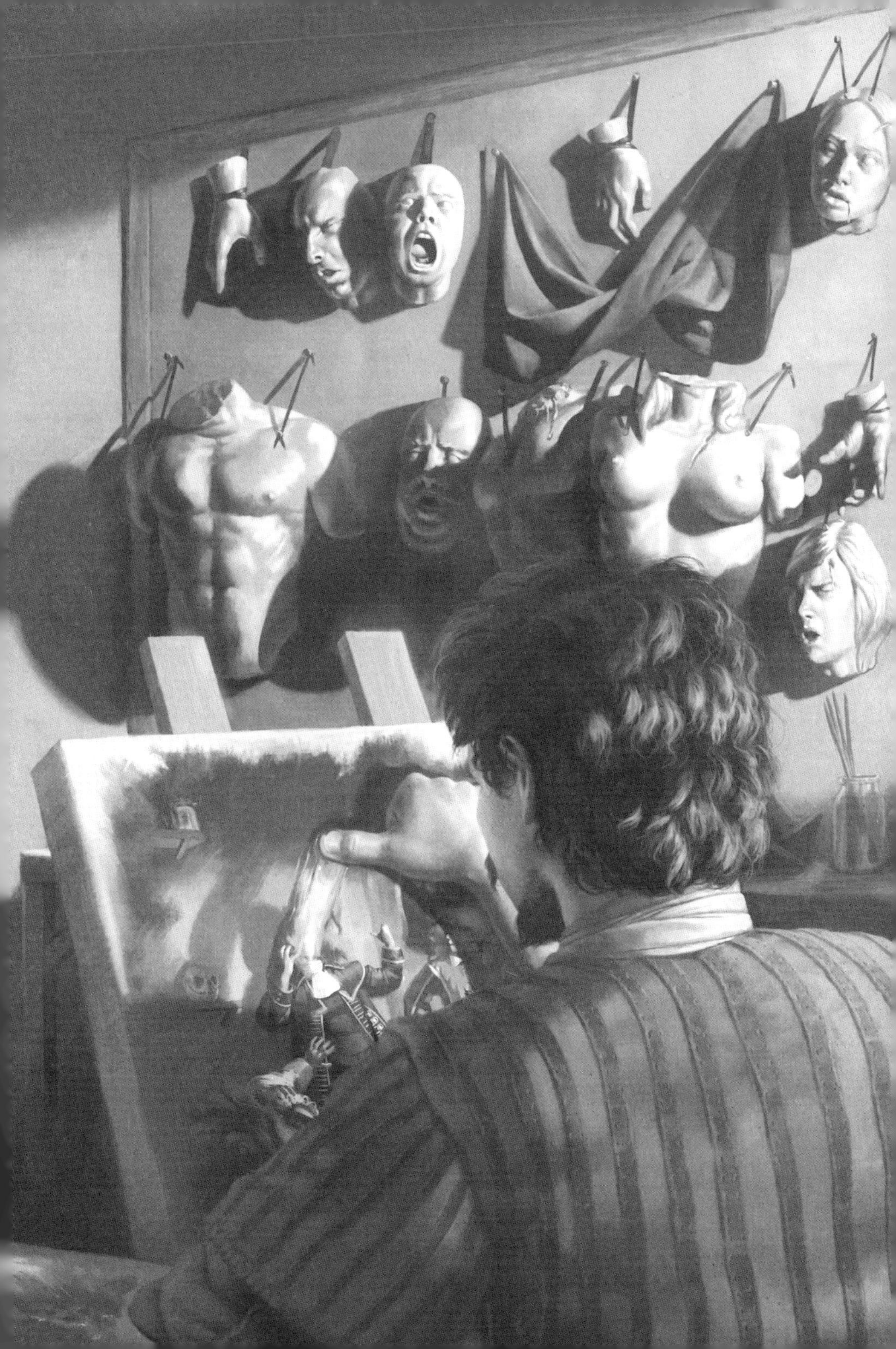

LAMENTATIONS *of the* FLAME PRINCESS
ADVENTURES

THE MAGNIFICENT JOOP VAN OOMS

Written by James Edward Raggi IV

Edited by Matthew Pook

Cover Art by Jason Rainville

Illustration, Cartography and Graphic Design by Jez Gordon

First Printed in 2012

CONTENTS

THE UNITED PROVINCES & AMSTERDAM

In 1567, sparked by religious and taxation issues, the Seventeen Provinces of the Low Countries rebelled against their Spanish rulers, beginning what history calls the Eighty Years War. In 1581, the Provinces declared independence, but the war raged on. The end result was a splitting of the Low Countries, with the northern portion becoming the independent United Provinces (more or less in present-day Holland) and the southern Spanish Netherlands remaining, for the moment, under Spanish rule.

The Provinces were already a major commercial hub before Spanish rule as they were a convenient stopping point on the European sea routes between the Baltic states, England, and Spain, and on continental Europe itself with neighboring France and major areas of the Holy Roman Empire, either by land or river. After the revolt, the United Provinces became pioneers in capitalistic practices, with Amsterdam establishing the world's first stock exchange (originally for the sole purpose of handling stock transactions of the Vereenigde Oost-Indische Compagnie, aka VOC or United East India Company or Dutch East Indie Company) and central bank at the beginning of the 17th century.

Dutch ships are common on the sea lanes, particularly in areas where the Portuguese—themselves under Spanish dominion at this time—officially claimed a monopoly, such as Brazil, Africa, India, and Southeast Asia.

Socially, the United Provinces are incredibly progressive for their day. The government is set up as a republic: the United Provinces are also known as the Dutch Republic or Republic of the Seven United Netherlands during this period), although this was more theoretical than actual. Representation for each of the individual provinces was decided by traditionally powerful landholding families and major business concerns, and the Princes of Orange as a hereditary line, tended to hold unofficial executive power. This was primarily because for the almost entire first century of their existence, the Provinces were at war—first with Spain and Portugal, later with England for mercantile supremacy—and a definite leader was called for.

While all of the country's major commercial hubs are more cosmopolitan than the ruling regime would prefer, the United Provinces nevertheless again took the lead in terms of tolerance. While the official religion of the United Provinces was Calvinism (which was a major factor in the break from Catholic Spain), Catholicism was not outlawed and churches of different denominations could be found in the same city. There was also a very different attitude towards class consciousness in the Provinces than elsewhere in Europe.

As far as most outsiders were concerned, the Dutch were scandalously permissive and promiscuous, in almost most every way. This is not to say that from a 21st century perspective that the United Provinces was a tolerant society, as attitudes towards, and tolerance of, different groups varied from one year to the next, and from one region to the next, most notably between urban and rural areas. Even they were also Protestants, Lutherans in particular had a difficult time establishing churches, and Jews, while not persecuted by the state (itself an incredibly forward-thinking step), could not establish official places of worship, even when granted official sanction, because of interference from other religious authorities and popular protest. Nevertheless, by the standards of the day, the peoples of the United Provinces were remarkably tolerant of other cultures and faiths.

The Dutch were also innovators in terms of military tactics. The "Pike and Shot" era of warfare was largely based on Dutch innovations on the battlefield, based on maximizing the effectiveness of the often-unwieldy matchlock firearm when combined with smaller sized and more maneuverable battalions comprised of pikemen, arquebusiers, and musketeers. The standardization of equipment as well as the training and drilling that these battalions required were a prime reason—along with the United Provinces' effective defensive siege warfare—why the Dutch forces were able to fight the Spanish (the most powerful empire on Earth at the time of the Dutch revolt) to a standstill and negotiate a truce.

Indeed, imitation of their methods would lead to militaries becoming more efficient and professional throughout Europe over the course of the next century and this would take a horrible toll on armies in the field in terms of battlefield casualties. *The Magnificent Joop van Ooms* assumes a present date of 1615, six years into an arranged twelve year truce with Spain. The Dutch have established very few permanent settlements overseas as of yet, but this very year have built Fort Nassau in the New World, at the location of present day Albany, New York.

AMSTERDAM

If the United Provinces in general are a world leader in terms of progressive thinking and commercial power, Amsterdam is the engine that drives this machine, being the largest city of the United Provinces, and where all of the financial and political powerbrokers are located. Amsterdam in 1615 has a population approaching 75,000 people, and within the last five years has conducted a major expansion to its canal system and defenses. Nor will this be last expansion to either. The city competes with London not just as a center of commerce, culture, power, and influence, but for the bragging rights to be the de facto "Capital of the World"—in European eyes at least.

Where else but Amsterdam could a world-class talent and genius of a man like Joop van Ooms be born? And where else but Amsterdam would such a man live?

DOWN ON THE WHARF

AMSTERDAM ENCOUNTERS (D50)

1 A group of poor children swarm around looking for hand-outs. One of them is a pickpocket who will attempt to pilfer something (Sleight of Hand skill 1d10-4, minimum 1).

2 A vagrant offer to sell them what is in his box for 1gp, sight unseen. Inside the box is the Hamster of The Hague, which can fit an infinite amount of matter in its mouth. If word reaches the Hamster of Amsterdam, it will not like hearing of its colleague's enslavement.

3 A ship is leaving soon and it needs fresh hands now. A press gang of 3d10 toughs decides that the player characters are fresh enough.

4 A drunken brute of a man (Fighter level 1d8) mistakes a player character for somebody that owes him money. A lot of money.

5 The Preaching Prostitute is looking to tell her customers that they are going to hell while providing her services.

6 Spanish spies are looking for collaborators. The player characters look capable and do not look Dutch, so would they mind helping out with a plot or three, would they?

7 Spanish spies are looking for collaborators. The player characters look capable and do not look Dutch, so would they mind helping out with a plot or three, would they? A-HA! These are actually Dutch spy-hunters looking for threats, and if any player character agrees to help the "Spanish," it is to the gallows with you now!

8 Everybody dies. Seriously. Roll up new characters, start them somewhere else. Amsterdam is wiped from the face of the Earth.

9 Drunken sailors looking for a fight. There are 1d10+2 of them, each a Fighter level 1d12-6 (minimum 0).

10 Drunken sailors looking for drinking partners. The player characters face a choice; party with them until dawn, or it is time to fight. There are 1d10+2 sailors, each a Fighter level 1d12-6 (minimum 0).

11 Completely sober sailors are looking for stimulating intellectual discourse. And by God, the player characters do look stimulating. The player characters must spend the day discussing philosophy and politics with these fellows in an upscale public house, or these men will make disparaging remarks about them all over town to the point where they suffer a -1 reaction roll penalty for the next week.

12 A fancy lad, just having completed finishing school, is looking for his father's ship.

13 A fisherman snagged some sort of golden trinket in his latest catch and is looking to sell if off before anybody catches on. It is worth 1d100x20sp, but he will part with it for half its value.

14 "Hey! This area belongs to the VOC! Show us your permits and papers!"

15 A prominent citizen, whose career would surely end if his activities here were known, is prowling the docks looking for a good time. One of the player characters looks like a sporting and discrete gentleman...

16 A beautiful woman is looking for a lover and wants to take a most handsome gentleman back to her place. The catch is that she is a mermaid and she most enjoys holding on to her love as he goes into convulsions as he drowns...

17 Smugglers are not always bright or well-prepared; a cart full of just-unloaded cargo breaks, spilling the crates' contents all over the place. Guns and powder!

18 Smugglers are not always bright or well-prepared; a cart full of just-unloaded cargo breaks, spilling the crates' contents all over the place. A strange beast in a cage is revealed.

19 A man running away from someone barges into the player characters. Panicking, he gives them the documents that he is carrying and runs off. The documents reveal the names of a dozen high-placed Spanish spies. Spanish agents arrive momentarily.

20 A man running away from someone blunders into the player characters. Panicking, he gives them the documents that he is carrying and runs off. The documents reveal military secrets belonging to the United Provinces. Dutch agents arrive momentarily.

21 A Portuguese slave ship is just in from Africa and it is over quota; not as much cargo perished en route as expected. The ship's buyer did not have the warehouse space to house all of the cargo and the ship's captain is looking to find a buyer for the rest. Anyone want to buy some cheap labor in its physical prime?

22 A fisherman snagged some sort of golden trinket in his latest catch and is looking to sell if off before anybody catches on. It is worth 1d100x20sp, but he will part with it for half its value. Unbeknownst to all, it houses an ancient evil.

23 Competing pamphleteers assail the player characters, selling their screeds about morality, news of the day, politics, war, philosophy, the proper way to train a dog, etc. Each pamphlet costs 1sp apiece. It will not satisfy any of them to simply buy their particular pamphlet, it is also important not to buy anyone else's.

24 Catastrophe! An out of control vessel slams into the docks, its powder magazines exploding as it does. Each character must make a saving throw versus Paralyzation or fall into the water, and then another saving throw versus Breath Weapon or take 1d12 points of damage.

25 A man dressed in black and obviously up to no good emerges from the water and climbs up a ship's anchor chair/mooring line. Do the player characters get involved? If so, what is going on? If not, what did they miss?

26 A young man introduces himself as a doctor's assistant. He is collecting vials of blood for medical experiments (he has 3d6 full vials on him already). He offers 5sp to anyone who will donate a vialful of blood.

27 A large ship is in the process of un/loading, and someone has left a cannon right there. Nobody is going to pay attention for another half hour in case anyone wants it...

28 Plague panic! The plague has struck again in London – or Lisbon, or Venice, or Stockholm, or wherever – and thorough inspections of passengers from those places are being conducted at random. And don't the player characters look like the very type to have come from there...

29 A man approaches the player characters as if he is an old friend, shaking hands, slapping backs, etc. He has actually stolen something that he shouldn't have and is attempting to plant it. His Sleight of Hand skill is 1d12-6, minimum 1.

30 Customs officials with armed guards are making spot checks for contraband. The player characters are not carrying anything illegal, are they?

31 A battered and bloody ship's captain has been assaulted by "extortionate criminals" and needs assistance getting his property back. Surely the player characters would help for a bagful of silver?

32 An assassin in the employ of an old player characters' enemy (or perhaps one that will be revealed in the near future?) strikes at one random player character. The assassin is a 7th level Specialist and has Stealth 6 and Sneak Attack 5.

33 A man deep in debt needs to sell his ship now. Half price, good deal, yes?

34 A nervous merchant confides that underlings have *gasp* smuggled something on his ship, and now he is fearful of being caught and prosecuted. Surely some rough looking customers like the player characters ("no offense") would be more of a mind to buy and take responsibility for such an item? (It turns out to be a real Egyptian mummy!).

35 Warehouse fire! And it is too close! The warehouse is already spewing smoke everywhere... and opium was stored there. Lots and lots of opium.

36 Older prostitutes, with their children in tow, loudly proposition the player characters. "You don't want to send us to the poor house, do you? Think of my kids!" (and this scene is being observed...)

37 Recruiters looking for people to join their exploration expedition to the New World/ Indonesia/India/Brazil to raid native treasures. Want to come? You get a full share!

38 In the distance, the player characters see an old enemy of theirs, one they know that they killed, but it is just a momentary glimpse and the enemy quickly melts into the crowd...

39 The player characters spy a body in an alley. Although grievously wounded and covered in blood, the victim is not quite dead yet, and if anyone tries to help he will snap back to lucidity and remembering his circumstance scream bloody murder before passing away... which will attract attention.

40 Weapons inspectors! Local authorities are concerned with violence in the shipping districts and so are confiscating arms and armor from those that do not have license for them.

41 Bumbling porters drop the crate they are carrying and it falls at the player characters' feet. It shatters, releasing the dozen deadly, aggressive vipers inside.

42 A man wants the player characters to sign a petition to clean up the filth in the harbor. At the same time, a group of jugglers approaches wanting money for their entertainment skills. The petition is actually a sign-up sheet to sign on as a VOC soldier overseas, and the jugglers are a distraction to get them to not read the document before they sign!

43 A ship has just come into port and it has had a rough time; only a few of its crew survived the journey. They need help unloading the ship by dusk (or dawn if it is already dark) or else the ship incurs extra fees. Would the player characters help in exchange for some random crate from the ship? If they do, at the end of the job—which takes right up to the deadline—they get a crate that ends up containing goods worth 1d12x500sp.

44 A ship has just come into port and it has had a rough time; only a few of its crew survived the journey. They need help unloading the ship by dusk (or dawn if it's already dark) or else the ship incurs extra fees. Would the player characters help in exchange for some random crate from the ship? If they do, at the end of the job—which takes right up to the deadline—they get a crate that ends up containing goods worth 1d12x5sp—the rest of the contents are all broken.

45 A performing monkey on a leash does some tricks and its owner wants money for the performance. He will threaten to kill the monkey if there is no money forthcoming. He will do it, too—he has extra monkeys at home.

46 Two very short men, one with a long beard, and one tall skinny man, approach the party and attempt to recruit them on their quest to destroy some hidden evil in the mountains of Norway.

47 A merchant carrying various elixirs in a case attempts to sell these "miracle" cures to anyone and everyone. They cost 5sp apiece, and there is a 1% chance that one actually cures diseases or heals 1d6hp of damage.

48 Lightning strike! One random character takes 1d30 damage and all equipment is burned to a crisp.

49 "Hey you lot! Not from around here, eh? Then you want to buy some genuine Dutch wooden shoes, which I coincidentally can provide! What size are your feet? Ahhh, healthy, ain't ya? Try these ones..." There is a 25% chance that the shoes have termites, and a 25% chance that they are an extraordinary set of shoes.

50 The player characters stumble onto an impromptu Beer and Cheese street festival, where they will be invited to partake in as much as they want. If they do, they will lose 1d6x10sp as they spend some money on useless trinkets and wake up the next morning in some strange place with a killer hangover, and if they do not, some friendly drunks are going to make sure that they take a swim in the harbor before they go about their business.

THE BLACK MARKETS

Amsterdam is one of the most important trading cities in the world at this point, if not the greatest. An incredible amount of cargo and merchandise passes in and out of its harbor and warehouses, a good deal of which is smuggled. This is a good place for player characters to buy and sell contraband.

When selling loot on the black market, the price paid will be lower than what the sellers would receive through legitimate channels (even after taxes!), but there are a good many items that are sold that would raise too many questions if sold openly. An attempt to sell loot requires a 2d6 roll, Charisma modifiers applying (use the Charisma modifier of the character whose player takes the lead here, not necessarily the modifier of the character who the players want to modify the roll):

SELLING ON THE BLACK MARKET (2D6)

1	The buyers are offended, and demand the item as compensation and payment equal to 25% of the item's value. Refusal results in the seller being attacked. (3d4 Fighters of 1d10-5 level each)
0	The buyers are offended, and demand the item as compensation. Refusal results in the seller being attacked. (3d4 Fighters of 1d10-5 level each)
1	The buyers pay 30% of full value, but puts out the word of what was sold and who sold it. The player characters have a 100% chance of meeting those wishing to eliminate them for possessing the item(s).
2	The buyers pay 30% of full value, but puts out the word of what was sold and who sold it. The player characters have a 75% chance of meeting those wishing to eliminate them for possessing the item(s).
3	The buyers pay 50% of full value, but puts out the word of what was sold and who sold it. The player characters have a 50% chance of meeting those wishing to eliminate them for possessing the item(s).
4	The buyers pay 60% of full value, but puts out the word of what was sold and who sold it. The player characters have a 25% chance of meeting those wishing to eliminate them for possessing the item(s).
5	The buyers offer to pay 60% of full value and if refused there is a 20% chance that the buyer will send agents to follow the seller and retrieve the items later, either through force or trickery.
6	The buyers offer to pay 65% of full value and if refused there is a 10% chance that the buyer will send agents to follow the seller and retrieve the items later, either through force or trickery.
7	The buyers pay 70% of full value.
8	Double-cross! The buyers attack to silence the seller(s) and take the item(s) for themselves. (3d4 Fighters of 1d10-5 level each).
9	The buyers pay 75% of full value.
10	The buyers pay 80% of full value.
11	The buyers pay 65% of full value and send word if anyone asks after the item(s) later.
12	The buyers pay 70% of full value and send word if anyone asks after the item(s) later.
13	The buyers pay 75% of full value and send word if anyone asks after the item(s) later.
14	The buyers pay 80% of full value and send word if anyone asks after the item(s) later.
15	The buyers pay 85% of full value and send word if anyone asks after the item(s) later.

If there is a particular item that the player characters want to buy (even magical!), the Referee must decide what the fair price is before proceeding, then roll 2d6, Charisma modifiers applying (use the Charisma modifier of the character whose player takes the lead here, not necessarily the modifier of the character who the players want to modify the roll):

BUYING ON THE BLACK MARKET (2D6)

-1	The item is not available at any price, but the sellers want 50% of its value for their effort anyway. Refusal to pay means getting roughed up by the seller's goons. (3d4 Fighters of 1d10-5 level each).
0	The item is not available at any price, but the sellers want 25% of its value for their effort anyway. Refusal to pay means getting roughed up by the seller's goons. (3d4 Fighters of 1d10-5 level each).
1	The item is not available at any price, but the sellers want 10% of its value for their effort anyway. Refusal to pay means getting roughed up by the seller's goons. (3d4 Fighters of 1d10-5 level each).
2	The sellers are charging 10 times the item's normal value.
3	The sellers are charging 5 times the item's normal value.
4	The sellers are charging 3 times the item's normal value.
5	The sellers are charging 2 times the item's normal value.
6	The sellers are charging 1.5 times the item's normal value.
7	The sellers are charging the item's normal value.
8	Double-cross! The sellers attack to silence the buyer(s). (3d4 Fighters of 1d10-5 level each).
9	The sellers are charging 90% of the item's normal value.
10	The sellers are charging 80% of the item's normal value.
11	The sellers are charging 75% of the item's normal value.
12	The sellers are charging 66% of the item's normal value.
13	The sellers are charging 50% of the item's normal value.
14	The sellers are charging 33% of the item's normal value.
15	The sellers are charging 25% of the item's normal value.

JOOP VAN OOMS

Joop van Ooms is polymath, working in Amsterdam as an inventor, architect, engineer, painter, poet, and sculptor. He was in his younger days also known for his athletic feats and martial prowess, but was injured in battle with the Spanish and now is merely average physically. His work has made him one of the richest men in Amsterdam, although he spends most of his wealth on improving the city.

He is a celebrity in his native Amsterdam, promoting himself as, and being acknowledged as, a new generation "Renaissance Man," recalling the intellectual achievements and artistry of the Italian greats. Ooms (and his last name is always referred to, by himself and others, as "Ooms" and not "van Ooms") publicly calls himself "the new age Da Vinci," and tends to make disparaging remarks towards other famous intellectual contemporaries—Galileo and Kepler, most notably—for their lack of artistic talent and other creative celebrities—Shakespeare, Jonson, Vega, Rubens, Caravaggio, and so on—for their lack of scientific acumen.

More controversially, he is an extreme advocate of peace and tolerance. He openly states that Catholics and Evangelicals (Protestants) have no reason to quarrel, that Jews should be full members of society, that the Christian world should pursue peace with the Ottomans and that Muslims are no less God's children, and that the natives of Africa, the Americas, India, and China (most notable examples) should be seen as masters of their own lands, and explorers and merchants as only guests when visiting their lands. He credits his experiences as a soldier and sailor for informing these attitudes.

Most controversially, while not a vocal proponent of such, he has been caught in scandalous same-sex pairings, although has defended such acts as "practicing the methods of the knowledgeable ancient Greeks and thus gaining insight into the life and times of Plato, Aristotle, and Socrates."

His flaunting of social mores has earned him many enemies, and most of his attitudes would have had him burned at the stake for heresy, beheaded for treason, or otherwise "officially" murdered. However, his affected personality as an eccentric artist earns him some leeway, as does his more-than-generous contributions to both the local religious authorities and civic projects, in terms of both money and work. He tends to spend his money on civic projects that his fiercest critics support, which results in the lessening of the ferocity of the criticism towards as well as providing support for a most eclectic array of projects. This has not gone unnoticed; pamphleteers and priests and politicians now often rail against Ooms, not because he has done anything to offend them, but because they wish him to spend money on their pet causes. He sees through most of these attempts.

Joop is, of course, a most gregarious person, yet does not seem to have any trouble finding time to both attend many social functions and to concentrate on his work. And he produces a lot of work. Many suspect that he secretly employs a small army of skilled professionals that does the work he merely signs his name to; how else could he be so prolific?

But all of this is the public face of Joop van Ooms. His secret—which he hardly keeps secret, it is just that everyone he tells privately treats it as a great secret—is that as a consequence of his studies and experiments, he has broken through to the Void Beyond the World and has seen both the glories and the feculence of creation. Where others react in horror or take a nihilistic attitude after being confronted by the Pointlessness of All Things, Ooms instead sees that all of the stuff regarded as so important by his fellow man just... isn't. Religion, nationality, sexuality, identity, none of it matters, so why so much pain? Yet he knows that nothing can protect him should he fully disclose his knowledge; the Church, the State, and seekers of esoteric and forbidden knowledge will descend upon him and devour him (figuratively or literally, depending on who it is that reaches him first...) if he were to tell all that he knows.

And so he lives, and works, spreading the ideas that he think he can get away with, and working subtly to undermine and destroy those who think differently. Mankind will be free!

Joop van Ooms: Magic-User level 6 (no spellbook and no prepared spells, however). Cha 18, Int 18.

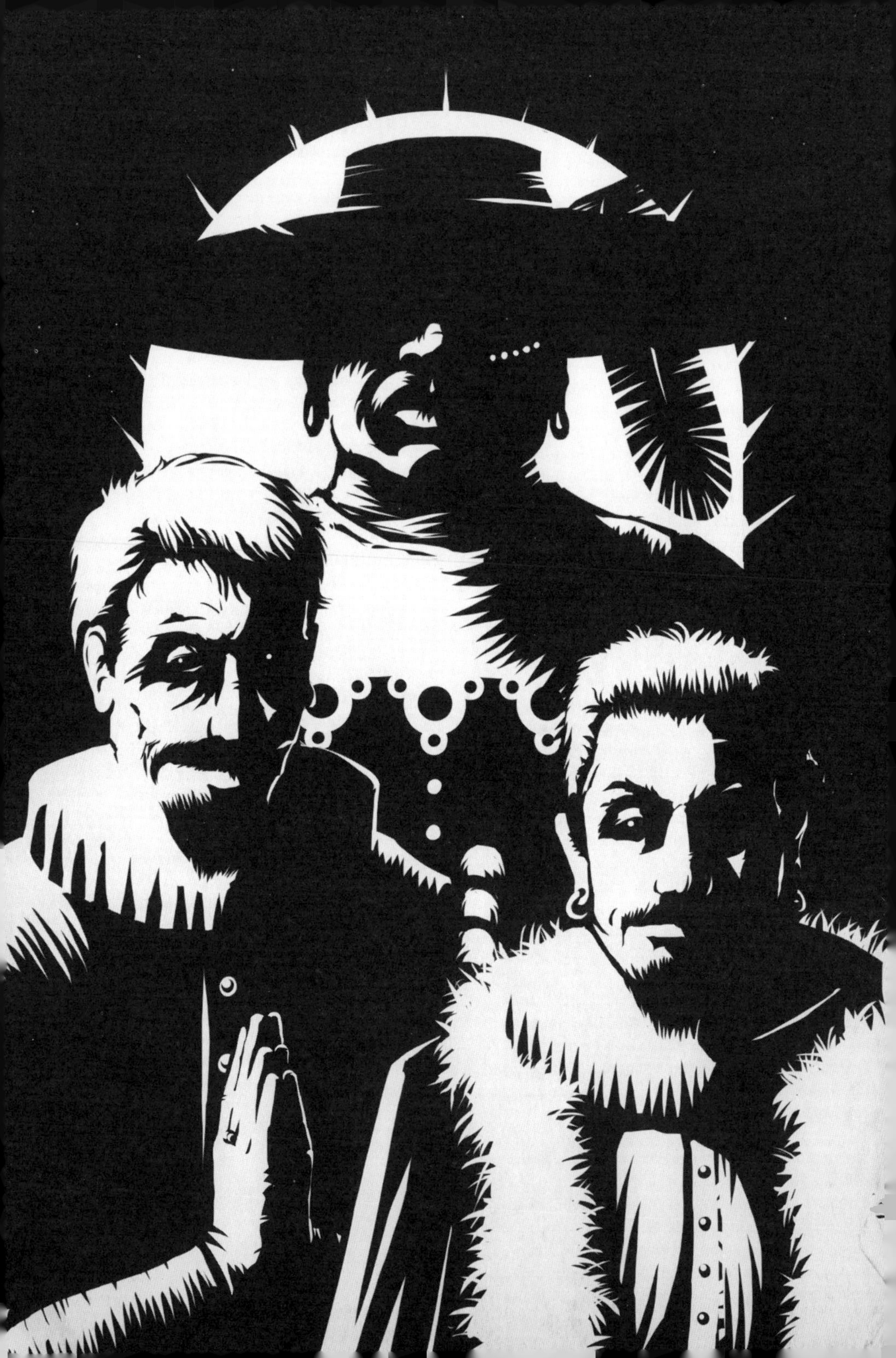

GILLES DE RAIS

Rais was a slave purchased by the Portuguese from sub-Saharan Africa some years back, but never took to the slave mentality. His masters beat, tortured, and mutilated him (he has no tongue and has been castrated, among his numerous other scars), but even this did not break his spirit. The slave eventually killed one of his handlers during an escape attempt, and for this he was to be publicly executed. But Ooms purchased the slave, with payment consisting of promises of a custom portrait and the designing of a new villa outside Lisbon, plus bribes for the local magistrates so that he could even buy a condemned and murderous slave in the first place. (Rais' former masters are all dead now from mysterious causes.) Joop then freed him on the spot. And offered him a job.

Rais is a giant of a man, massively built and as strong as a bull—this is the reason why his former masters gave him so many chances. This though, is not why Ooms employs him. Gilles de Rais' job is to hurt anyone that threatens the artwork of Joop van Ooms or the artist himself. In that order. For this Ooms pays him extravagantly.

Rais is a man in his 60s who has wanted nothing but peace his entire life, yet it has been denied to him time and time again, both in his native Ndongo and in Europe. Ooms knows that Rais will only act if it is necessary, but if he needs to, his bitter past will ensure that the actions he takes are swift and brutally final. Ooms gave the name of Rais to the former slave as something of a bad-taste joke, since he is quite capable of slaughtering those much younger than him as if they were helpless children. Besides, Rais is illiterate and so can never reveal his true name, and he had to be called something. And if both the name and Rais' demeanor intimidates people, so much the better.

Those that have partied with Ooms know that Rais can more than handle his liquor and keeps everyone involved safe. His dancing, a combination of his traditional tribal dances and contemporary European styles, makes many women very disappointed that he has suffered certain specific injuries.

Rais is always impeccably dressed, keeping up with modern fashions to a degree that confounds even Ooms.

Gilles de Rais: Fighter level 9, Con 15, Str 17.

HENRY VIII

Henry VIII (real name Geert Bogaers) serves as personal secretary, assistant, professional and social manager and all around lackey to Ooms and Rais.

He acts in a most effeminate manner at all times, but this is because he thinks it makes him seem more French and therefore appealing to sophisticated ladies. That he is often quite swift to comfort the ladies that are disappointed by Rais' disfigurements is what led Ooms to call him Henry VIII, for what else could you call such a ladykiller?

Ooms often treats Henry cruelly (in terms of pranks and inconveniences, never physical abuse), but only if there are witnesses. No point without an audience, correct? Henry is often very frustrated by this, but he puts up with it because at the end of the day, he gets paid well and Ooms always gets him laid, so what is a little egg on the face (literally) every once in a while?

However, to boost his self-esteem, he treats everyone not of the Ooms household with disdain, as if he is high-born and they are nothing more than excrement walked in from the street, and he tolerates no backtalk. He will block access to Ooms if not accorded the respect that he thinks he deserves, and Ooms will always act offended if someone attempts to meet him without going through Henry first. There was a famous incident at a state gathering where Henry told the Prince of Orange to go to hell for some imagined slight, and Ooms later refused to see the Prince until all apologies had been made to Henry.

They live dangerously.

Henry VIII: 0 level human.

THE STUDIO

Joop's home is a small tower in the center of Amsterdam, and is a public example of his architectural skills. The following notes about the house just note unusual items; everyday things are not mentioned. Note that Joop does not keep cash or valuables (besides his art) on premises, as he keeps most of his assets in the Bank of Amsterdam and authorizes payments through that institution. He also has a lot of wealth tied up in the Amsterdam Stock Exchange. If he needs cash quickly, he can always paint it. Note there is no kitchen nor dining area in the house. Joop believes that both attract vermin, and so he has food delivered every day at regular intervals, paying for it whether anyone is home or not. Any leftovers are thrown into the nearest canal as waste and the empty trays are left outside the front door to be picked up at the time of the next delivery.

LOWER CELLAR

The submarine (see page 15) is kept here (A). The doors opening into the canals are always kept locked.

UPPER CELLAR

Nothing is currently kept in this oddly shaped area (B) other than several kegs of beer and a wine rack. The door to the outside is always kept firmly bolted and locked.

GROUND FLOOR

The Sitting Room (C) is where Henry VIII spends most of his time when not out on errands or accompanying Rais and Ooms somewhere. This is also where Ooms will initially entertain first time guests to find out if they are interesting company or not.

The Guest Room (D), fitted with one large bed, is for any guests not staying the night in either Joop's or Henry's bed.

The Gallery of Minor Works (E) is just a small exhibition of things which Joop considers to be just "practice" pieces, though any one of them would amaze the layperson. The exhibits include cityscapes, portraits of women, small sculptures, that sort of thing. Anyone can tell that Joop is good from just these examples, and art experts will recognize that he is very talented.

The Empty Library (F) is a grand room full of empty bookshelves. Ooms does not allow books to stay in his house, and he wants people to realize just how brilliant he is rather than how brilliant his book collection is. "I read them, they're memorized, they're gone!"

FIRST FLOOR

Joop's bedroom (G) is almost bare except for the wardrobe full of clothes. He never sleeps here.

Gilles' room (H) is fairly spartan. While he keeps up with the latest look around others in order to fit in, at rest he is more comfortable not bothering with pretenses.

Henry VIII's room (I) is kept absolutely spotless and ready to receive the ladies. He keeps his clothes and a small stash of books here.

SECOND FLOOR

This floor is two stories tall. It is filled with trees and all sorts of plants that cannot possibly grow indoors as there is very little direct sunlight. Visitors will discover that there is often moisture reminiscent of recent rainfall on the plants and on the floor.

THIRD FLOOR

This is Joop's Museum, where he places his serious unsold paintings. Notable are:

- (J) A mostly finished painting which shows Joop himself swinging by the neck from the gallows while meteors rain down on Amsterdam, causing apocalyptic levels of destruction. A corner of the painting is unfinished, but as Ooms will point out, "If I ever die, the painting will be as finished as it ever could be. I wonder what will happen then?"
- (K) A nighttime landscape painting of Amsterdam, with the planets in conjunction. Ooms will tell anyone viewing the painting that, "The dikes almost failed that night, let me tell you!"
- (L) A scene depicting the sinking of a large ship in the harbor. "The captain had cheated me in a deal, so when this happened you could imagine how ironic it was," with this Ooms winks.

FOURTH FLOOR

All of Joops' real work is done in the Workshop. This includes his sculpting (M), painting (N), writing (O) and most of his eating and sleeping as well (P). Tools of the trade are everywhere, including a pottery wheel and many jars of raw materials from which he makes his own pigments. There is always a half-finished painting or pieces of sculpture here.

ROOF

The helicopter (see page 14) is kept here, covered in heavy cloth.

THE STUDIO OF JOOP VAN OOMS

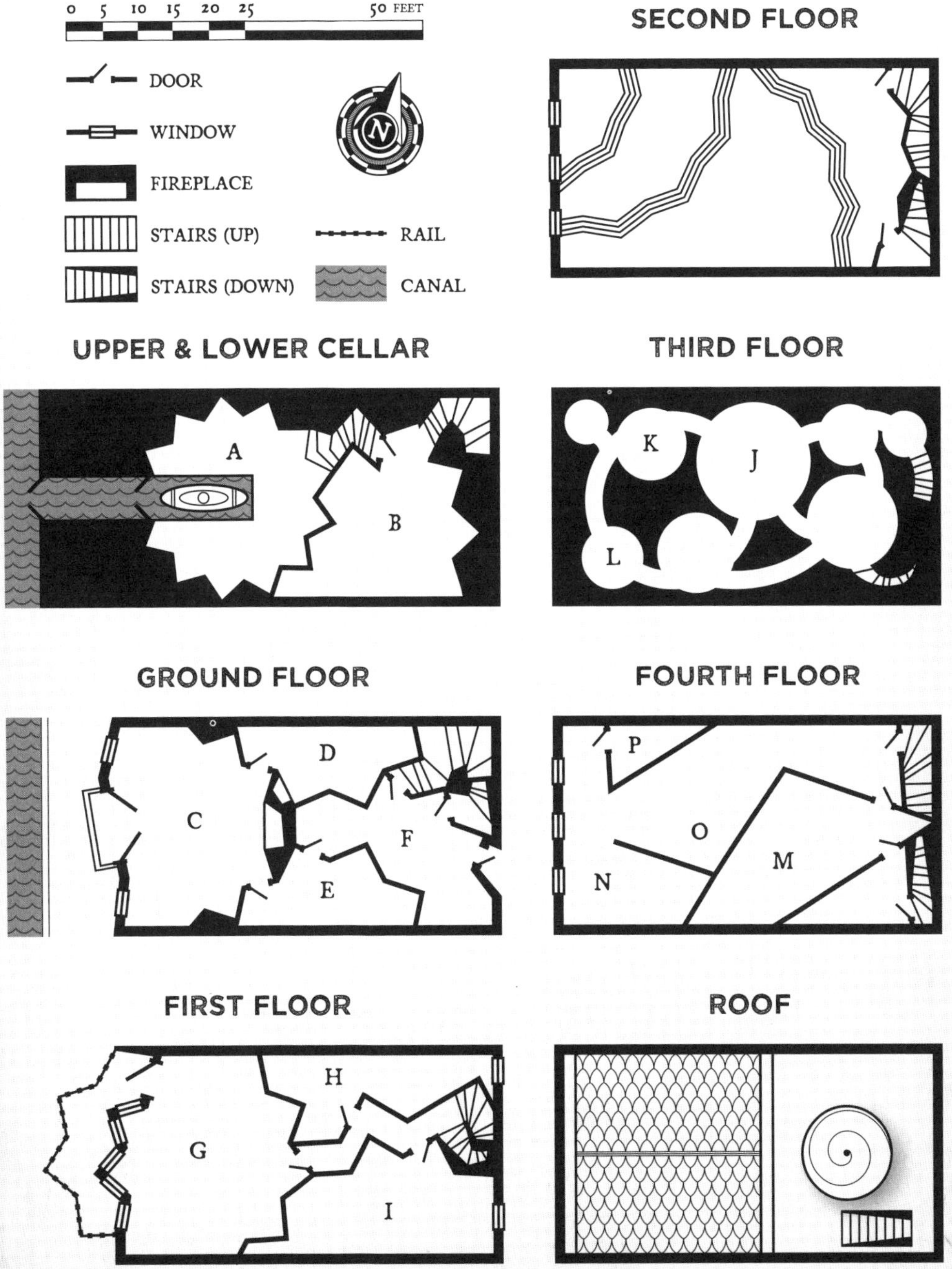

THE ART

Joop van Ooms is a world-class artist and creative genius in many fields, limited as popular gossip has it, only by what he cares to pursue.

ARCHITECTURE

Ooms is in great demand to design or remodel government buildings, churches, private residences, fortifications, and other structures. His style is to make a structure ordinary on the outside, extraordinary on the inside. Ooms does this, to the dismay of the rich merchant classes that wish to make ostentatious showings of their wealth, to force his clients to invite more people into their homes or their offices in order to show off the fact that they have paid for an Ooms design. Trademarks of Joop van Ooms' designs include:

- Star-shaped rooms (with any number of points, but eight).
- Six, seven, and nine, but never eight-sided, rooms.
- Asymmetrical rooms.
- Rooms with sloping ceilings and/or floors.
- Rooms with multiple raised and/or lowered sections of ceilings or floors.
- Walls, ceilings, and floors with patterns of holes in them, some holes big enough to stick fingers in.
- Tiled murals on walls, ceilings, and/or floors in abstract patterns which remind different people of different things.
- Rounded, cornerless rooms.
- Doors set in walls that lead nowhere.
- Strange acoustics which allow conversations in certain places to be clearly heard in specific other places elsewhere within the structure of the building.

As mentioned, he often undertakes design work pro bono to discourage his enemies. For those he reserves his most recognizable designs, allowing the owners of each structure to display its magnificence to all who pass by. But Ooms understands the subtle power of shapes, and some of these have terrible effects:

- Doorways which cause every eighth person passing through them to lose a random item most
- Gates which infect every eight millionth person passing through them with a deadly plague.
- Rooms in which anyone sleeping in them will quietly die the 888th time that they sleep there.
- Rooms in which every eighth person sleeping there will suddenly die eight days later.
- Rooms in which people will become seriously ill after every eighth meal that they eat there.
- Rooms which will sicken all within them if there are exactly eight people gathered there.
- Rooms which will cause one-eighth of all wealth stored there for at least eight hours to vanish.
- Rooms which will cause every eighth statue or other representation of a living being stored or displayed in them to come to life when no one is watching.

He reserves these designs for those who really annoy him. Ooms normally charges 1gp for each 10 feet cubed of the structure he is to design, payable entirely in advance. No refunds. Clients pay for style and bragging rights, not for actually liking the end result.

DRAMATIZATION

Ooms writes plays, albeit very strange and tightly directed ones. His "scripts" contain no words of dialogue, merely choreography (although he includes extensive explanation about what each individual movement, down to finger positioning, means), accompanied by the occasional great yelps inspired by opera singers (each play's instructions though, firmly forbids trained singers from attempting these). There are always exactly a dozen actors, each clad in identical, formless garb, involved in a production, but always only ever seven or nine, and never any other number, and never, ever eight, in the live performance area, designated by metallic gold paint spilled in some geometric pattern, at any one time. The "inactive" performers always remain visible to the audience, but stand outside of the live performance area.

As Ooms writes plays only for the most noble of humanist reasons, viewing one of Ooms' plays has beneficial effects —for the purely human. Each play has a different pro-human effect on the viewer (or the viewer's belongings), such as:

- Draining a level of any demi-human present.
- Removing any and all curses or conditions caused by extra-dimensional beings.
- Dismissing the prepared spells of any Magic-User present.
- Rendering blank any magical scrolls being carried by anyone in the audience.
- Granting immunity to any ill effects suffered from the viewing or reading of The King in Yellow, or similar anti-human entertainment media.

- Causing the complete and utter destruction of the next undead being to touch the viewer.
- Disenchanting any and all magical items within sight of the performers. Any part of the magical item has to be visible to the performers for this to take effect, so the grip of a magical sword will be visible, whereas a ring worn under gauntlets or kept in a belt pouch will not be.
- Giving immunity to the next Charm, or otherwise hostile psychic attack or supernaturally triggered insanity, suffered.
- The curing of all diseases.
- Curing baldness with rapid hair growth (this includes intentionally shaved areas).
- The erasure of all tattoos.
- Dismissing the prepared spells of any Cleric present.
- Rendering blank any Clerical scrolls being carried by anyone in the audience. This includes any religious text, such as the Bible, the Koran, etc.
- Complete immunity from sexually transmitted diseases until the next dawn.
- All carried ammunition is rendered useless, bowstrings break, powder becomes inert, etc.

Ooms directs every performance of his plays himself and oversees every rehearsal. For if they are not performed correctly down to the smallest twitch, each play will have a somewhat less desirable effect upon its audience. In the past, Ooms has had to hush up or invent scapegoats for mass strokes, rioting, all sorts of degenerate behavior, the simultaneous deaths of all a play's performers, concentrated lightning storms, spontaneous combustion (of the audience, the cats, and/or the theatre), the appearance of impossible monstrosities, and more, resulting from incompetent performances of his plays.

Ooms charges 200gp and requires ten weeks' lead time (plus expenses) to stage a production at a location of the client's choosing, but this also includes a surprise public performance, at a place and time of Ooms' choosing, of the same play. Ooms always chooses the play to be performed.

ENGINEERING

Ooms is a student of Da Vinci's works and strives to complete all of the things that Da Vinci designed, but never built... as well as a few other things.

THE GOLDEN GUN

Ooms' alchemical processes have revealed a way to turn a gun into a super-weapon—if the barrel is made of gold. The barrel must be made of at least 5000sp worth of gold in order to work as one of these super-weapons.

Ooms has one such gun in his studio. It is worth 10000sp and has a rifled barrel. The gun ignores all armor and does 1d100 damage, but each shot discharged destroys 1d00% of the barrel's value. Gold cannot stand the stress of a gunshot being discharged, and the chemical reaction of the exploding gunpowder reacts with the alchemical reagents needed to make the gun, corrupting the essential matter involved.

THE HELICOPTER

On the roof of Ooms' home is his helicopter. Assembled from lightweight materials that he had imported from Asia, the entire thing weighs merely fifty pounds even though its rotor blades extend to a twenty feet diameter.

In flight the helicopter's maximum speed is equal to the pilot's Strength score x 100' per turn if flying in a straight line or other steady pattern.

Whenever any maneuver (turning, descending, landing, ascending, etc.) is attempted, the pilot's player must roll 7 or more on 2d6. This roll will be modified by either the pilot's Strength, Constitution, or Charisma modifier, randomly determined each time that the roll needs to be made. Sometimes it works by sheer force, sometimes the pilot's endurance matters, and sometimes the thing works by sheer force of will. If the roll fails, the helicopter drops 1d10 x 10' and the pilot's player must roll again to stabilize the aircraft. Control rolls are made at a penalty of -1 for every level of encumbrance that the character has.

Operation of the helicopter requires both hands and both feet. If a character needs to use a limb for something else while in flight, a control roll must be made immediately, with a -1 penalty for every limb engaged in the operation of the aircraft.

After ten checks (successful or not), the pilot receives a +1 bonus to all checks in the future, although rolling a natural 2 always fails. The helicopter provides no protection against attacks. If the rotor blades are used as a weapon (and maneuvering in a position to do so requires a control roll), they do 1d20 points of damage on a successful hit. The rotors are likely to break; the pilot must make a saving throw versus Breath Weapon to prevent this with a -1 penalty to the roll for every point of damage inflicted by the rotor blades. If the rotor blades stay intact, the pilot must still make a control roll immediately.

If the helicopter crashes, it has an x in 10 chance of being destroyed, with x being the distance of the fall in tens of feet.

Ooms never flies the thing, considering it too dangerous for actual use at this point. He intends to design better sooner or later, but he keeps it here as both a prototype to improve upon and as temptation for theft. What army would not want an air force? Of course, were any army to steal and attempt to take it to war, it will only end in falling. Lots of falling.

THE SUBMARINE

In the basement, which has a hatch that opens onto the canals of Amsterdam, Joop keeps his latest technological marvel: a submarine. While not the first of its kind—English designs are known to a few, although it will be several years before they are made public—it is by far the most advanced.

The basic form of the sub is a wooden frame carefully lined with treated leather. In comparison with the English designs, it is huge and fits about ten people. Even a cursory examination will reveal that while the design allows for it to be towed by a larger boat, it has oars for maneuvering. However, it appears to be totally blind as there is no apparent way for anyone inside the submersible to see out.

Hidden panels (requires a Search roll; the inner leather lining of the sub hides the hidden features) reveal much more, however. A hatch in the floor allows individuals to slip in and out while the craft is submerged without flooding the compartment. Each rower station has a panel in the floor below which are pedals attached to small flippers that allow the craft to be propelled and maneuvered without oars (5' movement rate per pedaller). Hidden panels at the pilot's station open to reveal crude controls that open valves to allow water to flood several large bladders along the submersible's underside, while nozzles allow bellows to be used to push the water back out, allowing the subaquatic craft to submerge or ascend. Through the front area of the submarine's frame has been affixed a spyglass, which is the only means to see out of the vehicle. It is not a practical voyaging craft quite yet.

PAINTING: PORTRAITS

Joop van Ooms is a master with oils on canvas. His paintings are so lifelike that they almost seem as if what they depict is going to jump off the canvas. While Joop's artistic talents are not themselves supernatural, the result of a finished work is.

He never paints what he sees in front of him; what he paints is what will be at the exact moment that the painting is finished. He does not feel that he is creating this situation—although he totally is—so he does not feel responsible for the end result. He just "follows his muse." Because of this effect, he never shows anyone a painting until it is finished, and then it always has a rather significant surprise for the viewer. For a pretty lady or dashing fellow, he might paint a valuable piece of jewelry on them, which will suddenly appear. He might paint them in more extravagant clothing than they were wearing, which again will appear. A homely subject can be painted a better looking appearance, one that the subject's real face will transform into. He even granted a portrait to a friend of his who was unable to have children with his wife. He arranged them just so upon their first viewing of the painting, and in their portrait he painted a newborn baby, and they have been raising her ever since.

While Ooms is often kind to the subjects that he paints, he can be malicious as well. Valuables can be left out, clothes can be made shabby (or made to disappear), physical deformities can be introduced (even limbs removed), and there was a famous case where Ooms faced official inquiry on why he sat and painted "The Death of Councilor Hoekstra" after the Councilor's collapse, instead of summoning help.

(Incidentally, Ooms first discovered his abilities when a wizard commissioned a portrait from him. The mage bragged about overcoming some supernatural beast he described in great detail—to make the story of his besting it all the more impressing—so Joop thought it would be fun to depict this creature right behind the wizard in the painting. When it appeared, the creature slaughtered the wizard, and showed Ooms the true nature of creation, he thought it was even more fun than he anticipated!)

Ooms paintings are something of a fad right now in elite circles throughout Europe, but the degree of interest in any particular piece is unpredictable. Any particular painting sells for 4d10x4d10x1d4sp.

PAINTING: FRESCO

Whatever, and whoever, he paints on wet plaster disappears from the real world, becoming trapped in the fresco. Ooms has only attempted this in several extravagant merchant houses and government buildings, in the process "snatching" pets, violent vagrants, and annoying children away and into his scenery.

Since the local churches are Calvinist and thus do not contain devotional imagery, he has been sending messages to Roman Catholic archdioceses in French and German lands seeking permissions to express his religious devotion—in a manner that offends neither Catholic nor Evangelical sensibilities—by being allowed to decorate any newly built church with his talents. He wants to see what happens when he paints Jesus, God, and other Biblical figures on the walls. He would never do so in his own house—tacky, or in some public place where the art might be defaced or destroyed... if these entities do become trapped like mortals do, Ooms figures that their wrath after being freed will be too much for him to handle.

POETRY

Ooms is a prolific poet, perhaps not world-class, but his crowd-pleasing tendencies give him a popular following nonetheless, and also serve to make him a target of less popular, but more skilled poets.

Ooms does have the ability to move time with enclosed rhyme quatrains (four line poems with an ABBA rhyming scheme). Whenever he recites one of these, the time-shift contained in the quatrain happens, assuming that the subject is within earshot of the recitation.

This can move a person or thing forward or backwards in time, and it moves them back in their timeline. So if someone is moved thirty minutes back in time, they end up where they were thirty minutes ago, retaining full memories from the moment from when they were shifted in time, but it really is thirty minutes ago. The things that the time shifted person did—or will do—in those thirty minutes are not undone though. Nothing changes, but where that person is.

This is how Ooms gets so much work done without ever seeming tired; he timeshifts and works through the night, every night, several times, and then sleeps as well. Each time he wants to shift backwards in time, Ooms declaims the following quatrain:

"After another long day I yawn/Yet there is always more to be done/So accomplish I will more a ton/ So again I see this previous dawn." Effective if not impressive.

It must be noted that Ooms rarely timeshifts living beings into the future. For himself, he knows that someday the world will end, be it from the exploding sun or an encroachment of alien beings, but he does not know when. It could be any minute now! Ooms does not want to see it any sooner than he has to. As for others, he does not know what lies in their future, but were he to send anyone forward in time, it likely that they would be pretty mad at him once he caught up to where they were sent, so he does not do this.

The quatrain must be specific in naming the subject and the time-shift effect, so must really be made up on the spot in order to succeed. However, Ooms does have another one that he often uses a few minutes into a meeting when one or more private guests bores him: "Oh dear Lord you (all) are such a bore/ Such intellectual vacuousness fills me with nausea/ Yet carrying this conversation alone shall give me a hernia/So take ten minutes to gather your thoughts and try once more." Offenders will find themselves where they were ten minutes previously.

SCULPTURE

While able to sculpt with some skill, Ooms does not much bother. The magic only happens under the most macabre of circumstances. He must sculpt a hollow statue of a specific person or other being (and he likes to get plaster castings made of certain body parts), which he accomplishes by sculpting smaller pieces and then fitting them together. When that being dies, he must insert a portion of their remains into the hollows of the statue and then complete it. When this is done, it captures that being's essence and Ooms can communicate with this essence, asking one yes/no question of it per day.

Ooms' sculptures, when they are available, sell for 1d20x500sp.

ADVENTURE HOOKS

Every detail of Joop van Ooms' life and work can be turned into adventure hooks; that is the very point of *The Magnificent Joop van Ooms*. In all likelihood, the following examples are far less interesting than you as the GM can come up with:

The player characters are Ooms and similarly gifted artistic colleagues, living in a world of ignorance and cause-and-effect that would surely drag them down if they only knew...

- The player characters enter Amsterdam with some fanfare, perhaps after completing some quest which receives public attention. Joop wants to meet these new celebrities. Will they be interesting and persuade him to become a patron, or will they be ordinary and bore him so that he desires their removal from his brainspace?

- While on a distant coast or beach, the party finds a message in a bottle. All that is written on it is an Amsterdam address. It turns out to be Joop's, and he is thrilled that it has been found! He will offer to paint a portrait of the intrepid finders of his note and give it to them for free!

- Joop van Ooms is in a panic! He has heard rumors that someone has discovered the script of one of his early plays and that is going to be performed. It is not one of his mature, "good for all mankind" pieces! The party, being professional troublemakers, is contacted by Joop who offers generous rewards for a mission. They must find out who is doing this and put a stop to it! Who knows what will happen if the play is performed? Or if it is performed wrong?

- Robbers in the countryside have been using flying machines to commit their banditry. Who has armed these foul brigands, and why? The trail leads to Amsterdam...

- They have had enough! After one particular debauched party involving the perhaps-a-little-too-young sons and daughters of several influential merchants, Ooms has been seized and is headed to the gallows. Gilles recruits "independent contractors" to stage a daring rescue, because if Ooms dies, the current portrait that he is painting will technically be finished...

- Ooms is a fancy-pants rich artist whose work is worth tons and his house is right there! How much trouble could a robbery be?

- Entire ships are going missing from the harbor overnight at the same time that giant murals of those same ships are appearing on walls around the city. Investigation can lead only one place, but Ooms, if his secret is discovered, will claim that his latest batch of pigments has been stolen. Is the power in Ooms himself, and if so does he have a grudge, and if so, what do all these ships have in common and why is Ooms involved? Or is the magic in the pigments, and if so, who is doing this?

- It's August the 8th and Joop van Ooms has just died. His prophecy has come true, and thousands of meteors rain down on the Earth. The devastation is total and complete. All characters must save versus Breath Weapon or take 1d100 damage; those shielded from the effects face a burnt-out shell of a world where nothing grows, and the atmosphere has been damaged to the point that there is no protection from the sun's radiation. Everything on the planet perishes within a week. That's right. Rocks fall, everybody dies.

- "I'd like someone to find a certain something in the wreckage of the *Mary Rose*. I can get you there..."

- Ooms coughs while reciting a quatrain and sends himself centuries back in time. His only hope to return is to send a series of messages to the future... the first of which of course is discovered by the player characters. Do they follow the trail? Can they?

- Someone has remodeled an Ooms-designed building. It now has eight rooms in all and all hell is now breaking loose in that house. Ooms will not be cooperative even if contacted about the house; he thought the owner to be a real prat, doubly so now for screwing with Ooms' creation.

- Ooms really overdoes it one night and while piss-drunk paints surreal landscapes and unnatural events. The world has gone crazy... who can find the source of this oddity and convince him to fix it?

- Ooms goofed, and the latest building that he designed has created a pattern within the city that has opened portals that should not be opened. He is painting them closed, but how long can he stay awake to do so? Someone else is going to have to survey the buildings, decide which one is the best candidate for demolition, and then blow the damn thing up—over the violent protests of whoever owns it.

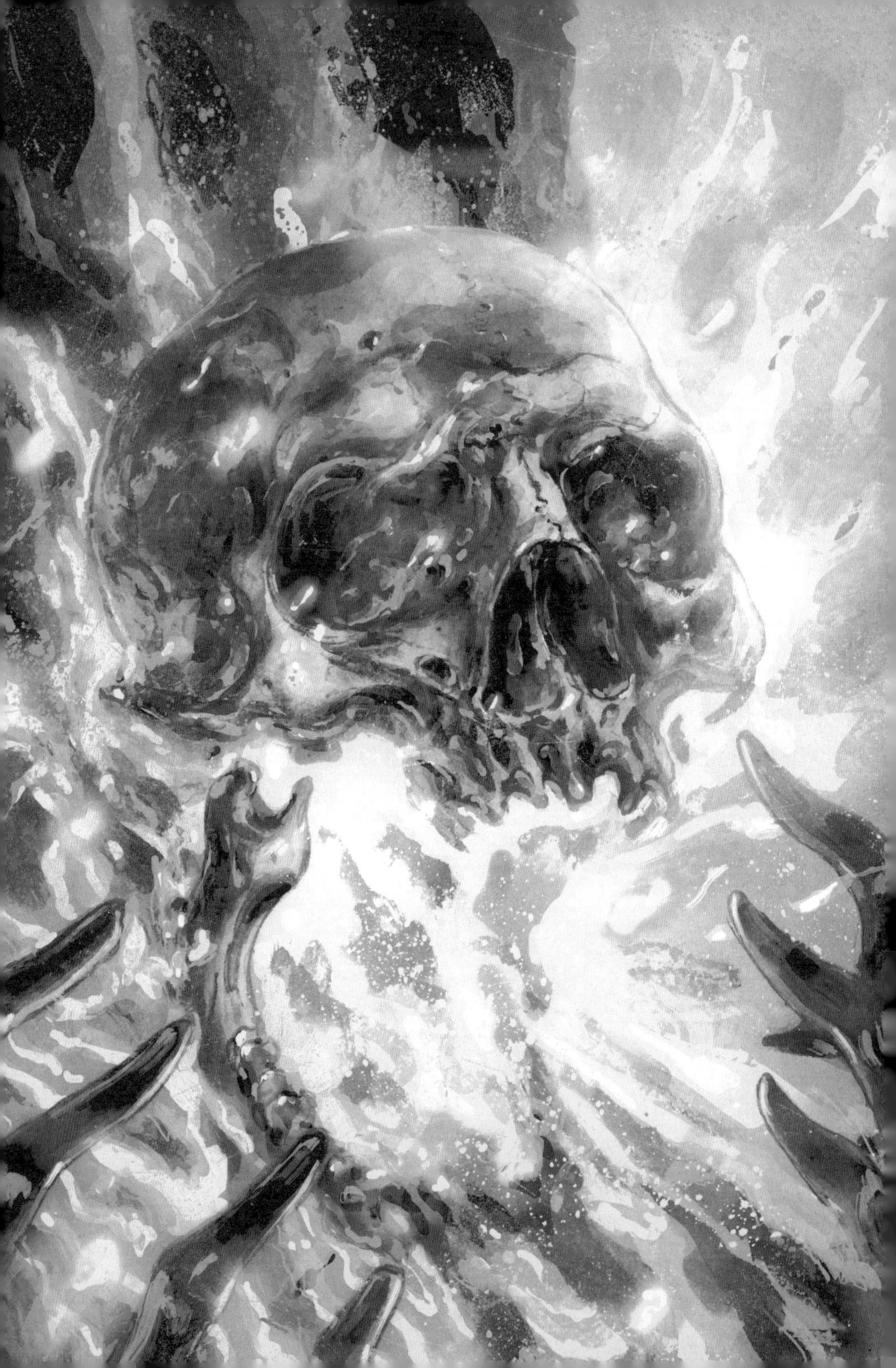

LAMENTATIONS *of the* FLAME PRINCESS
ADVENTURES

Fuck for Satan

Written by James Edward Raggi IV
Edited by Matthew Pook
Cover Art by Olli Hihnala
Illustrated by Olli Hihnala
Cartography, Illustration and Design by Jez Gordon

First Printed in 2013

Author's Notes

As I write this I'm still unsure whether or not I'm actually going to call this thing *Fuck For Satan.* It would be unnecessarily divisive and provocative, especially for an adventure that's essentially a farce, but honestly isn't that half the fun? So much crazy stuff happens within *Lamentations of the Flame Princess* releases these days that isn't 'adult material,' but is still likely to twist the knickers of people who like to get their knickers twisted (check out the **Twinkling Star** section of this adventure), that by putting something so patently tasteless right on the cover they can avoid spending money on a product they won't like anyway. Plus they'll do it loud enough that they will entertain us all with their outrage that a role-playing game scenario is not to their tastes and help me with a little publicity to boot.

I bet BADD and all the rest in the 80s never knew that they'd be so inspiring all these decades later, eh?

Still, seeing as how this adventure is basically about the influence of a walking penis, a few words might really be in order.

The truth is, I'm bored. Coming up with an idea that is both interesting enough to follow through with and that makes me giddy with excitement anticipating the reactions of the buying public is not easy. I have a big note book full of things that might be exciting enough in play, but they aren't very exciting to write; and if I'm not excited writing it, you're not going to be excited reading it. And of course, while game supplements aren't meant to simply be reading material, I believe that if you're not excited reading it, the chances are slim that it will ever see actual play; plus with forty years of RPG material floating around out there, including so much stuff given away for free by its creators, competition for your playing time is fierce.

Professionally I want *Lamentations of the Flame Princess* releases to stand out from the crowd, practically I want to give people ideas they weren't going to have on their own (else what use are these things?), and creatively I want to blow your mind and melt your brain. I'm not going to get that done with orcs guarding pies in 10' square rooms, now am I? (There's a cool line delivered by Roddy Piper from *They Live* that explains why I exclude the hell out of middles.)

There's also a disturbing trend in gaming that some people are trying to stamp down on imagination and creativity by trying to position the fictional depiction of real-life bad things as somehow indicating support for those bad things or even being a lesser form of the actual crime depicted! I admit I have an unthinking, automatic compulsion to oppose those sorts, because I think that 'creativity' and 'safe mental spaces' are incompatible. So I draw upon my more wicked influences when producing my own work, instead of drawing upon my love for *The Princess Bride* and that sort of thing, because I fear if nobody puts his foot down and takes the time to produce material to terrorize these people, they'll win and it'll be that much harder for more serious work with this sort of content to get done.*

Not to mention I like watching people who make themselves suffer for no damn reason. For example, the best part of watching *Belle and Sebastian* on Nickelodeon as a kid was the fact that my brother would just cry his eyes out, bawling in a most embarrassing way, because he really thought they really were going to kill that dog every single episode. Similarly, watching people get worked up about the supposed immorality of what the printed ink patterns depicting zombies are doing in the *Lamentations of the Flame Princess* Rules & Magic book is hilarious.

So maybe I'm just an asshole.

---

* *No, I don't really consider this work to be all that serious. It's about the influence of a walking penis, for crying out loud. Go watch some* Happy Tree Friends *and leave me alone.*

And being an asshole is better than being considerate and respectable. While considerate and respectable are fine attributes in a person you actually have to be around, that's real life. They're not qualities present in make-believe that blows minds and melts brains.

So enjoy your walking penis, and enjoy the rest too.

And listen to Mercyful Fate, Hell, Portrait, In Solitude, Attic, Ghost, Black Widow, Coven, Blood Ceremony, Jess and the Ancient Ones, and whatever other 70s/early 80s style occult and Satanic bands you can find, because everything else is false.

James Edward Raggi IV
June 27, 2013
Helsinki, Finland

PS. If you bought this in print, you are entitled to the PDF version at no extra charge. Email lotfp@lotfp.com with your proof of purchase and you'll receive a download coupon. I mention it because there's a handout in this adventure which is much easier to print off than photocopying or tearing a sheet out of the booklet...!

Using This Adventure

This is a nasty little adventure for the *Lamentations of the Flame Princess* game, or whatever old school game the Referee is using, or whatever other RPG he feels like converting this to.

The adventure basically is about the fact that some kids have gone missing from the small Swiss village of Schwarzton, and the villagers want to hire some traveling adventurer types to bring them back if they are alive, and eliminate whatever killed them if they are not. Since there is not much setting detail besides 'village in the mountains,' the Referee can set this adventure in any setting, and any mountains, changing the names of the village and villagers to suit their new home.

Schwarzton is not described in much detail because it exists merely to spur the player characters to go elsewhere. All of the inhabitants are zero level, nobody is particularly important to the adventure as an individual, and encouraging the players or their Referee to spend a lot of time there seems wasteful. However, nothing is stopping the Referee from fleshing the place out and making it more interesting and worthwhile in its own right, if he enjoys that sort of thing.

Before running the adventure it is important for the Referee to realize that **Fuck For Satan** is basically a Shaggy Bear story. The villagers' problem is some missing kids. There will be talk of cults and haunted hills and the player characters will be directed to a dungeon which will turn out to have absolutely nothing to do with the missing kids. However, you have to play that straight. "There are missing kids, villagers are convinced there's a cult behind it, and oh, here's a dungeon because dungeons introduced in these situations are where the solution to the problems are found." The point is that the Referee knows his players. He knows the tricks that will work on them,the ways you communicate what the adventure really is and what is just irrelevant in this adventure.

He should use that to get them there. He cannot, though, lay it on too thick. If the Referee is a bit too keen to get his players to go there, they might realize that something is up, and then he will never get to use half of the adventure. He should just try to imply that this is a shitty railroad adventure where the problem is presented, the location of the solution is suggested, and then if the dungeon is interesting then the session turns into an evening's worth of cool gaming, but oh boy what a 'an old man greets you in a tavern' lame level of setup and exposition.

Then once in the dungeon, the characters will eventually either all die or eventually figure out the kids are simply not there, but are nevertheless convinced they must have missed a secret door somewhere despite having completely mapped the place. (The Referee is advised not to laugh at either their efforts or their desperation.) Then the Referee gets to spring the other 'cult' on them and have them deal with the walking penis. The walking penis is much more hilarious when half the party has already died for no reason in the screw-you dungeon.* Well, hilarious for the Referee, but considering that his players probably run roughshod over his adventures half the time he has to have his fun sometime.

So even after the walking penis has turned up and been dealt with, the players will discover that this has nothing to do with the damn kids either. What kind of sadistic adventure is this, and what kind of crappy Referee are you for running it?

Or maybe this adventure might be wrapped up in 20 minutes of play with no player character casualties if the player characters do not take the offered bait or the random bear roll comes up a 1 right away. That is the chance that the Referee has to take really, or else that fun at his players' expense is not part of the give and take, part of the win and lose, part of a game—it is just abuse.

Oh, and lastly, it is best that the Referee not let his players know that he is running a published *Lamentations of the Flame Princess* adventure, and certainly he should not tell them the name of it. They will only get suspicious.

If the Referee must broadcast ahead of time what he is running (say, if he is setting up a Google+ hangout game), he should simply state that he is running 'The Schwarzton Incident.'

* *Although what I typically call the screw-you dungeon is still a possible low-risk windfall for a particularly clever or lucky party.*

Schwarzton

Schwarzton is a sleepy little village of about 50 families nestled in the Swiss Alps, its residents earning their keep mainly through farming and livestock. The region has not seen a war in over a hundred years and life has been good.

Unfortunately, in the last few weeks things have not been going so well:

- **20 days ago,** a meteor fell from the sky. That is never a good omen.
- **18 days ago,** Heinrich's only horse went missing from its paddock. It was assumed there was a passing horse thief since there was no damage to the fence.
- **16 days ago,** one of Hermann's cows disappeared from the barn.
- **15 days ago,** Stefan's St. Bernard, Hugh, went missing. It was a grand old dog, not one to wander far from the home, and no signs of its remains have been found in the area.
- **13 days ago,** one of Ulrich's sheep went missing from the flock. It was rather conspicuous by its absence because it had a nasty scar on one flank and Ulrich's daughter had felt sorry for it and thought of it as a pet, tying ribbons around its ears. She is most distraught about it. Again, there have been no signs of what happened to it.
- **12 days ago,** one of Lukas' biggest hogs went missing from the pigpen. Once again, there was no damage to the fence, no other animals missing, no sign of its remains, and no sign of a predator.
- The villagers had become increasingly worried about these missing animals, even posting watches around the village, but animals still went missing.

Then...

- **10 days ago,** the first child went missing. At first nobody connected it with the missing animals, because children often roam (it is not a dangerous region) and every so often get lost.
- **8 days ago,** the second child went missing, and that is when all hell started breaking loose in the village.
- **7 days ago,** villagers were sent to the nearest larger towns, even as far as Geneva, to scour the taverns looking for 'traveling adventurers' who might be able to help.
- The days passed, with no one coming to help, no sign of the children, but no further disappearances.
- Then **one day ago,** another child, not heeding the stern warnings about wandering off into the woods, disappeared.
- That was **yesterday,** and today is whenever the player characters come across the village.

How the player characters are introduced to the adventure depends on their current circumstances. If they are traveling through a mountainous region, perhaps this village just happens to be a convenient stop on their way, and its inhabitants will be a bit too overjoyed to find this heavily armed group of travellers passing through. If passing through a town near some mountains, perhaps they see an 'Adventurers Wanted!' notice or maybe an old man (the village will not send their productive young people out to do this) approaches them in a tavern. After all, this is a classic way to start an adventure. The plea for adventurers, when delivered outside of the village in whatever form, will be on the behalf of 'Theobold Bothe,' who "wants the return of family heirlooms." None of the announcements will contain any more information than this and certainly nothing as specific as to the nature of the assistance required or the fact that the village itself is responsible for the notice.

Whatever the approach that gets the characters to Schwarzton, once their prospective saviors are present the villagers will be much more forthcoming, telling them about the missing animals, the missing children, and the fact that Something Must Be Done.

Old-timers will then relate tales that their grandparents told them about an old Satanic cult that had a shrine in the nearby hills. The location of that shrine is now known as Old Haunted Hill and has been avoided by the villagers for generations now. In the wake of the disappearances, the villagers have begun to harbor the suspicion that the cult has somehow been revived, and consequently, they fear that the children have been taken for sacrifice. Despite these fears, the villagers are terrified of the place and will not go and see for themselves if their suspicions are correct. That is what the adventurers are for.

After hearing about the situation, some might wonder why the village has not contacted the real authorities in the region for help. They will receive one of two answers.

If the party shows any obvious religious affiliation, the answer will be that Schwarzton has fallen through the bureaucratic cracks of the Canton and pays taxes at an absurdly low rate. Raising the alarm here will bring both unwanted attention and long term difficulties as well as the desired immediate aid.

If the party does not show any obvious religious affiliation, the answer will be that since there is suspected Satanic activity, there is the fear that the 'assistance' will come in the form of state-sponsored yet independent witch-hunters or an official inquiry akin to the Inquisition. This the villagers know full well will endanger innocent lives when all the villagers want to do is to protect them.

Player characters will doubtlessly want some sort of reward. This is a simple agricultural village and they do not have much in the way of money. However, some of the single young ladies of the village would be quite enamored with those who manage to save the village from evil, and their dowries would include land and livestock. In actuality, several of the farmer's daughters are looking for husbands, traditionally minded as they are, but because they also crave some excitement, they are looking for husbands who they have not been around all their lives. Although the villagers will not put any pressure upon the player characters to marry their eligible daughters, the young ladies in question will be obvious in the crowds that gather around the newly arrived would-be saviors. Whether looking for love or land, the player characters can find it here. Female player characters might have a bit harder time of it, as becoming a young farmer's wife and not owning the land does not quite have the same luster. The villagers will be obviously gobsmacked that there would be women adventurers, and the young men of the village will preen and attempt to impress these characters as much as the village lasses attempt to impress the men.

The one thing that the village does not have to give as a reward is money. Schwarzton is not poor by any means, but most of the trade within the village is done in kind, and trade outside the village is usually conducted by barter, so there is very little cash floating around. However, some will point out that Satanists often worship golden idols and such things and whoever breaks up such a coven of evildoers surely has a claim on whatever treasures they find.

Of course, it is up to the Referee to figure out how to convey all of the important information to the player characters, and how that is done is dependent on the style at the individual table. Intensive role-play, or breeze over it so everyone can get to the 'real' adventure, or what?

Here is one suggested method:

The player characters are brought to the blacksmith's. Johann, the blacksmith, is a big, burly man fitting his profession.

"Oh, right, you want to hear about this cult? My dad knows about that. Daaad! DAAAAAAAAAAAD! You've got visitors! DAAAAAAAAAAAAAD! He'll be right out. DAAAAAAAAAD! Hurry up!"

A few minutes later, an ill-dressed ancient man arrives, spine curved horribly and staying upright only with the help of a knotty old cane.

"That's enough of that shouting! I'm old, not deaf! Now what do you want...? oh, strangers. What do you want? Don't you know how rude it is to visit unannounced? I see you're not from around here, which might explain why you don't have the good graces that God gave a worm. Well what do you want? Spit it out; don't stand there with a look on your face like a bee's just stung your bits. Spit it out!

"Missing young people? Yeah, I heard those rumors, but I wouldn't believe them. See, all those rumors were started by the shepherds out in the hills, and I don't trust those shepherds. They are not honest men. If they were, they'd work their land instead of just walking all over it. If you ask me, I think they're all just looking for an excuse to screw sheep all day long. Awfully suspicious that these people would disappear into the hills with no human companionship, hmmm? And they get so jealous when you touch one of their precious sheep. Yeah, they're always looking to say something that will distract you from the truth.

"But they say that some young people have gone out for strolls into the hills and have not come back. Some of the women around here just won't shut up with their wailing about their poor Jörg or Cordula or whatever dumb shit names people are giving their kids these days going missing. Well if they are, it's their own damn fault!

"People their age should be working all day, not going off for long walks. Certainly not with members of the opposite sex! My goodness, can you believe what young people do these days? In my day we had proper courtship! We'd look nervously across the crowd at each other during festivals, and then the man would work up the courage to go serenade the young lady underneath her window one night, only to find out it's the wrong window and you've scared the lass' younger brother to death so their father comes out and kicks the shit out of you. The mother gets worried that her husband's almost killed someone so they take you inside to nurse you back to health and it's the original girl's ugly-ass sister that takes care of you and BAM, you marry that one!

"That's how I met this useless piece of flesh's mother, and that's how it should be done."

At this point, Johann interrupts his father with,

"Daaaaad, it's kids. The little kids that have gone missing."

"Oh shut up boy, you're the worst blacksmith alive today, and you know it. The only reason you have the job is you're the only one with arms big enough around here to use a hammer at all. But your brain is too small to learn to do it properly!

"Where was I? Oh, these kids today. Back in my day, we never ran off to the hills to 'frolic' or whatever code-word these snots use today. For one, the hills were dangerous! All sorts of monsters and bandits and assorted evil kept us in our homes with

our windows shuttered tight when we weren't in the fields risking our necks to feed our families! 'The hills' were just another word for DEATH!

"Not to mention how improper it is! In my day, a young man would never be alone with a woman before marriage! You wouldn't even get to hold the woman's hand until your wedding day and you liked it that way because that meant you were being proper and honorable! Take this waste-of-life's mother, for example. You couldn't find a more frigid woman. We had marital relations just one time, on our wedding night, because she was proper and honorable enough to fulfil her obligations, and she kept telling me to hurry up the whole time!"

"Daaaaaaaaaaaaaad!" his son interrupts a second time.

"Oh shut up, boy! Your mother was colder than a yeti's balls and she was proud of it! And I loved her for it, because that's the commitment I made. Kids these days, they don't have that kind of respect. 'Oh, love is a natural thing, it should be given freely!' The very thought of it makes me sick! They were probably stealing off in the night to go elope to the nearest big town or something, because they don't care about proper standards or morals in those town things. Nobody in those places does a proper day's work, you know that? Here we work with our hands and we work the ground. In towns there are people that get paid to count things and write down what they've counted! Can you imagine? Getting paid to do that? That sounds like woman's work, if women would be allowed to have anything to do with money or business.

"So yeah, these missing kids, maybe they aren't old enough to be sinning like rabbits, but they would have been in a few years, because they're brats now, because they're parents don't raise 'em right. Brats I say! Probably just wandered off into the woods and were too busy eating their boogers to pay attention to where they were walking, and they're probably in Milan by now. The village at least has been a bit quieter since they're not around."

At this point, Johann injects more voluably with, *"DAD!"*

"But even a blind man hit's a bulls-eye once in his life so there is a remote possibility there is something to all this talk. I doubt it, because you know how women gossip, this is probably blown all out of proportion, but if these kids have been going missing for real... hmmm... I do recall years ago there was some trouble around here. My gran'pappy told me about it. Some group of Satan worshippers or another taking up on the Old Haunted Hill and causing trouble. You people don't look like you have any honest work to do so maybe you could trouble yourselves to take a stroll a little bit that-away and make sure everything's the way it should be – deserted!

"What? Reward? You want a reward for doing this? What kind of adventurers are you? Back in my day, you couldn't take two steps around these parts without tripping over some do-gooder who was begging to solve all your problems! 'Are there fair maidens in need of rescuing?' 'Is your cat stuck in a tree?' If you had a problem, the adventuring lads of yore would be there to help. They had honor. They had stones.

"Look around you. Look over there. What do you see? Fields. Over there. Look. See that? Pasture! And over there. Look closely. Hills! You want a reward? Really? We've got chickens, carrots, and milk. If you want to drive a hard bargain I suppose someone around here could give you some beets. We're a farming village you dolt! You think we have big piles of money sitting around just to give away to strangers? Don't be such an idiot!

"Think about it! Satanists – and it's always Satanists – are morons. Why else would they put on fish masks and dance around some idol in the dark? 'Ohh, oooh, I'm dancing and being blasphemous! I'm sooooo evil!' Why in my day I'd go give them what-for for the fun of it! I didn't need no reward! But say these youngsters have been kidnapped instead of just getting lost. These cultist idiots always have some sort of golden junk or another.

"That just proves how stupid they really are! Why, if I were young and aimless and without the good upbringing a farming village gives you and I came across a big hunk of gold, I'd buy some land. Gold can buy a lot of land, and a lot of security against bad harvests. I could provide for a large family quite easily for the rest of my life with a good chunk of gold! But no, what do

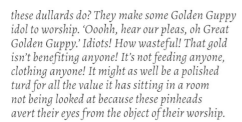

these dullards do? They make some Golden Guppy idol to worship. 'Ooohh, hear our pleas, oh Great Golden Guppy.' Idiots! How wasteful! That gold isn't benefiting anyone! It's not feeding anyone, clothing anyone! It might as well be a polished turd for all the value it has sitting in a room not being looked at because these pinheads avert their eyes from the object of their worship.

"Oh if I were only a few years younger, I'd march up them hills and kick all their asses just for being stupid! And then I'd kick all their asses again for messing with our young folk!"

"Oh, look at this. I've gotten all excited and I've pissed myself. And it's time for my nap. You'll be wanting to go past them hills there, there's an old shrine on a hill that these fishheads used as a home base years ago. Has some rocks on it, you can't miss it. My gran'pappy said that the geniuses around here said they burned the whole shrine down the last time there was trouble, but seems to me Satanic altars are made of stone. Stone don't burn!

"So you can prance up them hills and since you're all obviously greenhorns that don't know your asshole from a hole in the ground, you'll probably all get killed, but if not, and there are cultists, you bring some of them back alive, you hear? No need murdering them all through stealth, since you're probably too cowardly to stand up to those pricks in a stand-up fight. Get some of them back here so we can give them some good old-fashioned country justice! We haven't had a decent hanging around here in far too long!"

If the Referee likes this approach, Johann's father's rant is probably best delivered in the style of Grampa Simpson. But this should not just be read verbatim off the page! The Referee should memorise the key points and improvise in the spirit of the rant so the players remain engaged. Of course, if this sounds too silly, the Referee might to take a more serious approach to presenting the information, or alternatively draw inspiration from another source.

As long as the information is delivered, the particulars of the delivery are not important, although as the above approach suggests, they can be fun.

BONUS RANT FOR GAMES THAT USE DEMI-HUMANS:

"What? Rambling? Show some respect!

"I see you've got one of those pointy-eared bastards with you. Have you ever heard one of their poems? They take weeks to finish! I've been there, in one of those mosquito-infested parks they call a homeland. Lazy shits never mow their lawns, I tell you that! And we were the 'honored guests' for one of these songs or poems or whatever the hell it was. I think to this day it was a treacherous betrayal and an assassination attempt because I was damn near bored to death! 'Oh, look at me, I'm all skinny and ageless, but I have great sorrow and I will now warble on for six weeks about twigs and weeds and the majesty of the stick insect!' Don't you tell me I'm rambling, boy, you don't know the meaning of the word!"

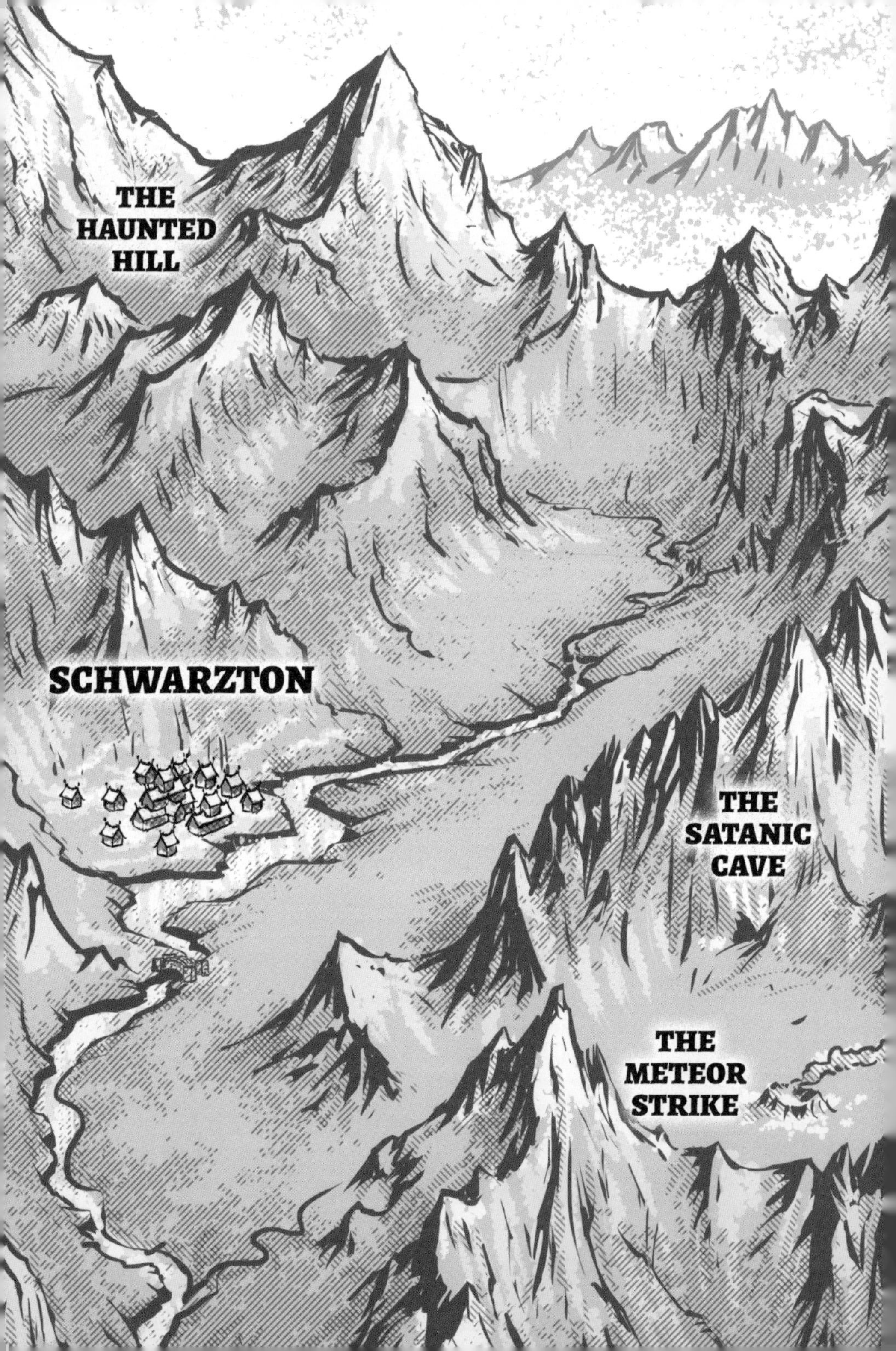
THE HAUNTED HILL
SCHWARZTON
THE SATANIC CAVE
THE METEOR STRIKE

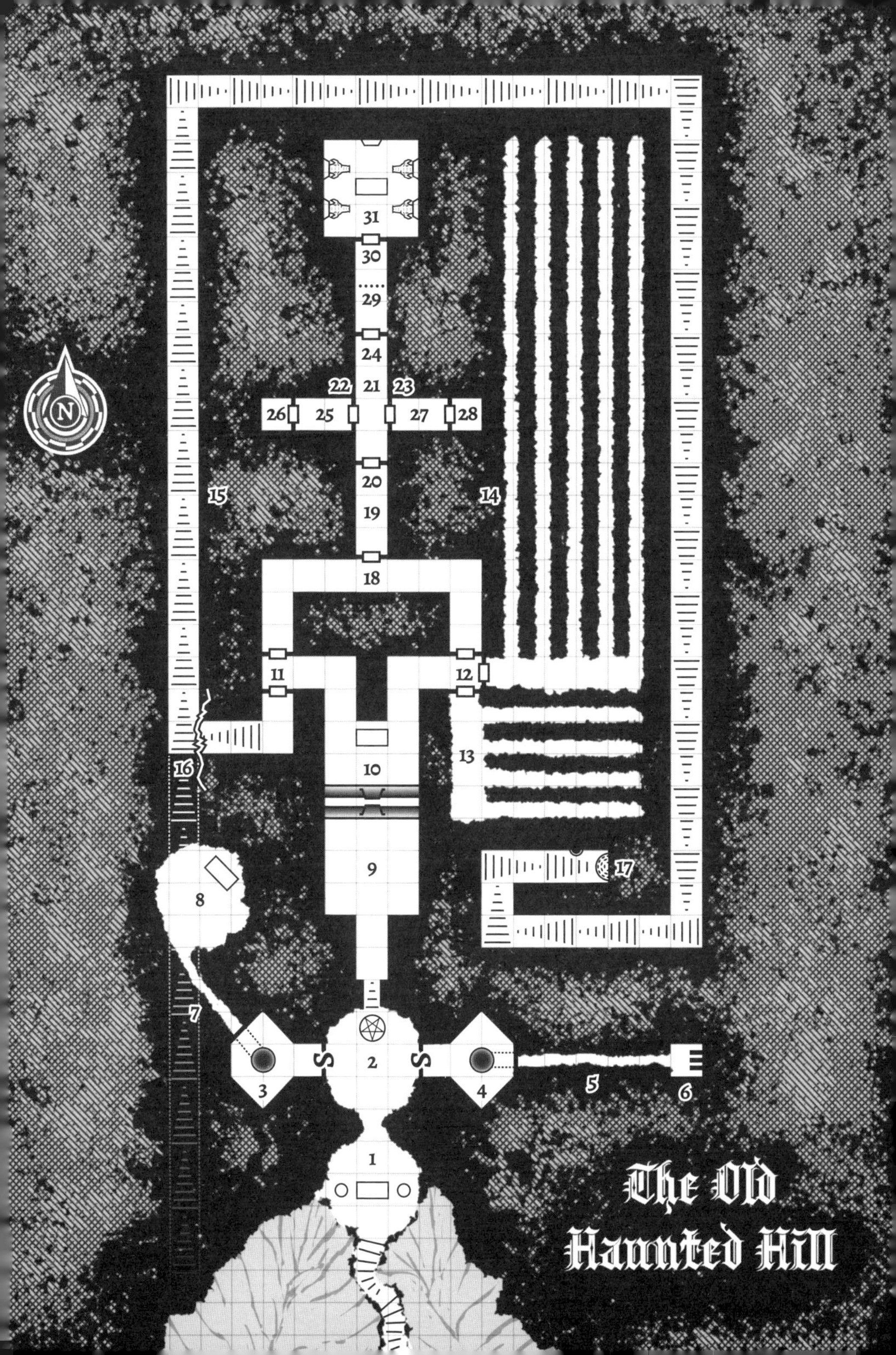

N
31
30
29
24
22
21
23
26
25
27
28
20
19
15
14
18
11
12
13
10
16
9
17
8
7
2
3
4
5
6
1
The Old Haunted Hill

The Old Haunted Hill

It takes about an hour to get to the Old Haunted Hill if guided there, or 1d6 hours if relying on the directions given by the villagers. Finding a guide is not so easy, as few want to even to be able to see the hill. For a fee, a goatherd will guide them to the Hill, but will not go up the Hill nor will he wait for the characters to return. The Referee should make an inverted reaction roll (so a roll of 2 is counted as 12) and multiply the result by 10 to determine how many silver pieces a guide would want just to show a party where the hill is.

Children can be more easily convinced to show the way, but the child would not be able to return to the village on its own, and trying to shoo the child away once reaching the Hill will result in the child going missing.

Taking the child up the hill and into the dungeon would also work if characters are fond of bad ideas.

If a child is enlisted as a guide, the villagers of Schwarzton will be forever hostile to the characters and all offers or intimations of marriage be withdrawn.

If the child does not return alive, the villagers will be violently hostile and will do all they can to see the characters dead.

The hill itself is rather steep and treacherous, but fortunately there is a staircase carved into the hillside which provides a convenient means of ascent.

1. The Altar

At the top of the stairs is a flat area not quite at the top of the hill. Before a cave stand an altar and two rough pillars, fashioned from stone not native to this region.

On the altar is a book entitled *Charting the Heavens*, an astronomy book written just the previous year. Tucked inside the front cover is a folded note – give the players the Handout if they discover this. (Note that Iri-Khan does not appear in this adventure, nor is there any information given to how he placed the book here ahead of the player characters' arrival. He is intended to be one of those annoying loose ends that infect a campaign on an on-going basis.)

If they follow the instructions in the letter, the player characters will find that the first letters of each section in the book identifies a particular star in the sky and advocates reciting a poem to it:

Twinkle, twinkle, little star,
How I wonder what you are.
Up above the world so high,
Like a diamond in the sky.

Give wisdom of future events,
Certain demise it prevents.
Knowing when I need know most
To conquer the cosmic host.

If this is done, then The Twinkling Star makes itself know to the player characters.

The Twinkling Star

Upon being identified and serenaded, one star in the sky will make itself known by becoming brighter and twinkling in set patterns. It will make it known to the one calling to it that it hates you.

Not the player characters. It likes them. It wants to see them succeed. It hates you, the Referee, the actual person reading this right now. It despises you and your willingness to kill innocent people for amusement. Sure, to you they are imaginary, but they exist in the same world as this star. Those people are very real to this Twinkling Star, and it is going to get back at you just to show you that cosmic horror does not just flow one way across that Referee's screen.

Now that you have read this, you must include the star's effect in your next prepared adventure. It does not matter who wrote the adventure, whether it is your own or something you bought or downloaded. If it is a prepared adventure, the star takes effect. If you do not like these effects, then you'd better just improvise sessions for the rest of your life.

(You might wonder what authority this adventure has in dictating to you how you should handle the next adventure in your campaign. This author pleads diminished capacity; the star got to me and I'm just forwarding this information on to you.)

Before you run the next prepared adventure in your campaign (not future sessions continuing or revisiting an adventure already begun!), roll on the following chart and submit to its instructions:

1. You must furnish the maps for all adventure locations in the adventure to the players as they enter them. No textual information need be on the maps, but the number keys must be on them. Each page of maps will be signed, "Against the cosmic tyrant, your friend, Twinkly."
2. You must inform your players prior to the start of the adventure that they have access to cosmic knowledge, and they may receive full and thorough and truthful reports on any three characters or items they encounter in this adventure. That is three reports for the group, not each player.

3. Forty minutes after play of the adventure begins, you must place your full and complete adventure notes in the players' hands. All maps, keys, written information, personal notes if running a published adventure. Everything. They have sixty seconds to look through them before returning them. Note that if you play online doing this may be a copyright violation. You need to choose... defy the law, or defy Twinkly. Caught between a rock and a hard place, eh? Not to mention you have no way of making sure the players all delete the material you show them after 60 seconds. Sucks to be you.

4. Every roll you make, even ordinarily secret rolls like secret door searches and the like, must be made in full view of the players. And no 'idly rolling the dice behind the screen to make players wonder if something's happening.' If there is to be a die roll, it has to be made in full view. And during the adventure, every player can declare their dislike for a Referee's roll once, and call for a re-roll.

5. Before play begins, players should email their character sheets to lotfp@lotfp.com. Using LotFP's internet access, Twinkly will alter one fact or figure on the character sheet, and that is now official in your campaign.

NO LONGER VALID

6. The NPC or creature with the highest level or Hit Dice in the adventure should have that figure reduced by half. Half of the subtracted levels or Hit Dice may be distributed to other creatures or NPCs in the adventure, but no more than 1 Hit Die or level may be added to any one creature or NPC.

This is totally going to ruin the adventure, right? Do not worry Referee, LotFP does not like being under Twinkly's thumb any more than you do. So tell you what. We are going to allow you to make your next adventure harder for the players. This adjustment does not have to be revealed to the players as part of one of the previous conditions! In case this adjustment does not apply to the adventure (if it mentions dungeon rooms and nobody goes into a dungeon, for example), you are allowed to hold onto it until it does apply. To determine how the next adventure should be made more difficult roll 1d10 (none of these changes apply to the Player Characters or their hirelings, retainers or allies):

1. Glass cannons – for your next session, switch everyone and everything's Hit Dice and Hit Points (with 0 counting as 1). So if you have a 1 Hit Die dog with 4hp, it'll be 4HD with 1hp.

2. One random placed monster (not one that's only on a random encounter table) regenerates all damage (even if killed, or disintegrated, etc) every round as long as it is exposed to light. (If killed in darkness, it doesn't come back to life if exposed to light after that.)

3. In the year 3227 a local bomb squad disposes of suspicious packages by transporting them backwards through time since their mathematicians have determined that the chances of harming anyone by doing so in 1 in 300,000,000,000; this is that one, so random likely foe of the PCs has the bomb inside, going tick tick tick, and when that creature dies the bomb will explode doing 5d6 damage to everyone within 30', 3d6 to 60', 2d6 to 90', (including appropriate damage to objects and nearby structures), save vs Breath Weapon for half damage.

4. The three largest treasure stashes in the adventure are adjusted down to the next less valuable coin type (gold becomes silver, silver becomes copper), and gems/jewels in those troves are worth only 1/2 as much as they are presently valued.

5. Every opponent in the adventure with 10 or more hit points has a 1 in 4 chance of having the hit point digits in the most advantageous order... so a creature with 18 hit points would instead have 81.

6. Any creature or opponent in that adventure with more than two hit points maximum that ever finds itself reduced to exactly two hit points is then instantly fully healed.
7. The largest treasure haul in the next adventure is reduced by half, and replaced with a doubling of the number of creatures or opponents that guard/own that treasure.
8. The enemy with the most hit points in the next adventure (or NPC/monster that you assume before the adventure fits that description) has a problem--it splits into two separate beings when it takes damage, both retaining its full individual hit points minus the damage that caused the split. So if you have a 40 hit point Fighter enemy that takes 5 points of damage, you now have two of them with 35 points. They will then take damage individually, but will continue to split. Each retains the mentality of the original. Something reduced to 0 or fewer hit points does not split.
9. Roll 1d10. That is the total number of "floating" Hit Dice you can add to any foe in the next adventure you run, at any time. Even if they've just been killed.
10. Every pile of treasure in the next adventure, and the value of every precious item, has its digits reversed if it lowers the value. For example, a gem worth 500sp is now worth 005sp... a pile of 362 silver coins is now 263 coins... but 25sp jewelry would remain at that value and 263 silver coins would stay the same, for example.

2. The Cave

This cave is littered with rocks and crawling with bugs. As characters wander into the room, a few of the more ornery critters will crawl, jump, and fly up the character's legs or between the legs and attempt to bite. If a character's legs and nether regions are not suitably protected (the Referee should ask exactly how their clothing and armor is fitted down there), the character must make a saving throw versus Poison or suffer a -1 to all rolls for 1d6 hours due to the resulting severe irritation.

The cave has one obvious notable feature: The statue.

The life-sized statue depicts a regally dressed man with a skull face. The top and back of the skull are missing and hollowed out, with a depression for an oil and wick. If a fire is set inside the head, the light shines out the eye sockets in a manner where the light falls on each of the secret doors.

The statue is quite heavy (being solid stone and all), but it is on a hinge; leaning it to the left reveals stairs descending down into the darkness...

The secret doors to the east and west are merely expert masonry designed to make the doorways indistinguishable from the rest of the cave wall. The doors may be lifted out of place (they do not swivel or pivot, they are more fitted boards).

3. The Dry Well

A well stands at the center of this hexagonal room. The well is 45' deep and a very narrow passage leads from the bottom. Anyone wanting to traverse the passage must strip himself of any arms, armor, backpacks, and so on, before squeezing his way into it and crawling along on his belly.

4. The Dry Well

A well stands at the center of this hexagonal room. The well is 45' deep and at the bottom, buried beneath rock and dust and bits of ancient debris and bits of bone, are a number of bear trap-like mechanisms. There is a 1 in 6 chance that anyone walking on this surface will set one off. Each has razor sharp serrated teeth that does 1d4 points of damage and holds the victim fast. A Sleight of Hand roll is necessary to successfully free the trapped character; a failed roll here forces the trapped character to make a saving throw versus Paralyze or suffer another 1d4 hit points of damage as the trap's jaws slams shut again. Each trap resets to an open position when the teeth in its jaws touch. For a character who gets a limb caught in the trap, the jaws of the trap will touch when he has lost both 6 hit points and the limb has been severed.

Rats and insects too slight to set off the traps infest the area, entering through cracks in the walls, and although living creatures can fend them off fairly easily, they will devour any who are caught in one of the traps and are unable to escape. They inflict 1 hit point of damage per hour to any character that remains here.

The passage leading from the bottom of the well is very narrow; a normal sized person can only squeeze through crawling on their belly after stripping himself of any armor, backpacks, etc.

5. Narrow Tunnel

This tunnel, so small that a normal sized person can only squeeze through by stripping himself of any arms, armor, backpacks, etc., and crawling on his belly is absolutely infested with insects. Small, bitey insects. A character crawling through here will be bitten so many times that he will be swollen and supremely itchy and irritated, causing -2 to all rolls, for 1d4 days unless extreme (magical?) measures are taken. There is a 1 in 6 chance that the crawling horde also contains a particularly poisonous insect, in which case the character must make a saving throw versus Poison or suffer 1d4 hit points of damage.

6. Levers

This is a standard 10' by 10' by 10' cube-shaped room. Its only feature is the three levers that stick out of the eastern wall, in the exact center of the wall. Each lever is at the centre position, but each can be pushed up or down. Moving the levers will have different effects, all accompanied by creaking metallic scraping noises originating from behind the wall:

Lever 1	Lever 2	Lever 3	Effect
Up	Middle	Middle	Deactivates the lock at location #18.
Up	Middle	Up	'Deadbolts' the door at location #18 so that it cannot be opened.
Up	Middle	Down	Deactivates the lock at location #20.
Up	Up	Middle	'Deadbolts' the door at location #20 so it cannot be opened.
Up	Up	Up	Deactivates the fire/acid breath trap in location #31.
Up	Up	Down	Deactivates the lock at location #22.
Up	Down	Middle	'Deadbolts' the door at location #22 so it cannot be opened.
Up	Down	Up	Deactivates the lock at location #23.
Up	Down	Down	'Deadbolts' the door at location #23 so it cannot be opened.
Middle	Middle	Middle	No effect; default position.
Middle	Middle	Up	Deactivates the lock at location #24.
Middle	Middle	Down	'Deadbolts' the door at location #24 so it cannot be opened.
Middle	Up	Middle	Deactivates the lock at location #30.
Middle	Up	Up	'Deadbolts' the door at location #30 so it cannot be opened.
Middle	Up	Down	Raises the bridge across the pit at location #9.
Middle	Down	Middle	Deactivates the lock on the northern door at location #11.
Middle	Down	Up	'Deadbolts' the lock on the northern door at location #11.
Middle	Down	Down	Deactivates the lock on the southern door at location #11.
Down	Middle	Middle	'Deadbolts' the lock on the southern door at location #11.
Down	Middle	Up	Locks the statue in location #2 in place so it cannot be moved.
Down	Middle	Down	Deactivates the lock on the northern door at location #11.
Down	Up	Middle	'Deadbolts' the lock on the northern door at location #11.
Down	Up	Up	Deactivates the lock on the southern door at location #12.
Down	Up	Down	'Deadbolts' the lock on the southern door at location #12.
Down	Down	Middle	Prepares the fire/acid breath trap in location #31 so that it activates as soon as the door to the room is opened.
Down	Down	Up	Flushes the basin at location #17 so no hearts remain in it. It does refill with inky black liquid though.
Down	Down	Down	The entire tunnel leading to this room collapses, as does the well structure in location #4.

With the exception of the last two, effects only last while the lever is in a particular position.

Note that searching for traps will only confirm that the levers do something; there is no way short of dismantling the entire section of the wall to determine that the levers are attached to a gearbox that connects to mechanisms that lead into the wall. Performing this dismantling deactivates the levers so moving them has no effect, and there is only a 1 in 10 chance that attempting to rebuild the gearbox would be successful.

The room is infested with insects, which will cause 1 hit point damage per hour that a character remains in the room.

7. Narrow Tunnel

This tunnel is so small that to traverse its length, a normal sized person must strip himself of his arms, armor, backpacks, etc. before squeezing through by crawling on his belly.

8. The Tomb

This rather non-descript cave has a loose sandy floor, so loose that any unencumbered person will sink to his ankles, while a heavily encumbered character will sink up into the sand up to his knees.

A sarcophagus, plain but for the carved Dead Sign on the lid, sits in the northeast corner of the cave. Inside the sarcophagus is a skeleton that has had every single of its bones broken.

Resting on the skull is a crown made of coral and lead (worth 2500sp). The skull itself rests on a very obvious pressure plate. Removing any weight from the plate (and this includes the crown!) causes the sand floor to become even looser, causing characters with any encumbrance at all to sink like a stone to a depth of 10', and unencumbered characters must make a saving throw versus Paralyze every round or sink, and can only 'swim' 10' a round.

Also among the bones is a stone key.

9. The Shrine

This long worship hall has a 10' wide, 10' deep pit bisecting it. The floor of the pit has numerous tiny holes in it. There are no obvious means of crossing the pit except for two 'bridge' sections that look as if they pivot up from the walls of the pit to form a safe means of crossing.

Unfortunately, both 'bridge' sections are securely held fast to the pit walls.

If the bridge sections are forced or otherwise improperly opened (see location #6 to discover how to properly open them), fire will shoot from the holes, burning anything in the pit, and burning anyone leaning over the pit for 1d6 damage unless they make a saving throw versus Breath Weapon.

10. Most Worshipful Altar

This stone altar is completely plain, but for the Dead Sign inscribed on it. On the altar is an ancient book bound in pigskin (but should give the impression that it is human skin). The title, *Prayers for the Dying*, is in the Duvan-Ku script and undecipherable without either a Language roll at -3 penalty or the use of a *Read Magic* spell.

The book is filled with prayers and hymns ("I worship death and hope to be an offering to the god of pain," and such like) written by a skilled calligraphic hand, but someone else has added marginalia on every page in the form of scribbled lines in rough red ink.

If anyone leafs through the book they will notice that the lines form a little animated pattern as the pages are flipped through. Anyone seeing what this animation is will indeed animate it, and the scribbles will rise from the book and grow into the fearsome Half-Realized Poorly Conceived Terror.

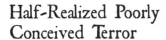

Half-Realized Poorly Conceived Terror

This tangled mass of ever-shifting, spastic and jittering lines and smudges and shadows, which is perhaps 10' long on each side, is a piece of aggressive art. At times, it is able to almost coalesce into a firmly rendered shape, albeit an unnatural and horrible shape. When it does so, it gives the impression of trying to solidify, although the reality is just the opposite. It rages at being 'alive' and will seek to eliminate all solid living objects, blaming them for its animated state. It wishes nothing more than to once again be nothing more than lines on a page.

Armor 17, Hit Dice 4, Movement 60', 1 squiggly attack doing doodle damage, Morale 12.

Its special abilities are as follows:

- It is completely immune to piercing weapons and projectiles. You cannot shoot a line, let alone a squiggly line!
- Crushing attacks and attacks with blunt weapons only do 1 hit point of damage if they hit.
- It is utterly impossible to grapple the thing.
- Its attack is not limited to mêlée range; it can attack any target within 50' with a quickly uncoiling line.
- Once per existence, the creature may 'breathe' a torrent of dotted lines which affect any creature within a 50' radius which fails a saving throw versus Dragon Breath.
- If it hits with one of its various attacks, the victim must make a saving throw versus Magic.
- If the save is successful, the Referee must roll 1d6 to determine the effects of the attack:
    1. The character's clothing is stained a conspicuous, ruinous blob of color.
    2. The line pierces the character's skin and gives a messy, prominent tattoo of rather indistinct composition.
    3. The character's eye 'floaters' become manic and distracting, giving the character -2 to hit and -2 to Search rolls for the 2d6 turns (this effect is cumulative; if a character gathers a -10 penalty to hit from this effect, his eyes explode).
    4. Any maps the character has in hand become meaningless stains. If the character carries no map, then the closest character with a map must make a saving throw versus Magic or this effect strikes that map.
    5. Bad perspective: The character is temporarily unable to judge distance, and will be -2 to hit with ranged attacks for the next 1d10 days.
    6. Still life: One object that the character touches in the near future will turn out to be a 'life drawing,' basically an illusion that does not exist. Any object the character touches has a cumulative 1% chance to be that object.
- If the save is unsuccessful, roll 1d6 to determine the effects of the attack:
    1. The weapon the character is wielding, or the main weapon the character carries, is reduced to squiggled nonsense and is destroyed.
    2. A random book or scroll the character is carrying is reduced to incomprehensible gibberish as the written lines scatter and fragment. If the character is carrying no such thing, then the squiggles enter the character's brain and the character becomes *Confused*.
    3. One of the character's limbs is reduced to stick figure status. Stick figure arms are not able to lift anything heavier than 5 lbs., and stick figure legs travel normally if the character is unencumbered, but any encumbrance points count double.

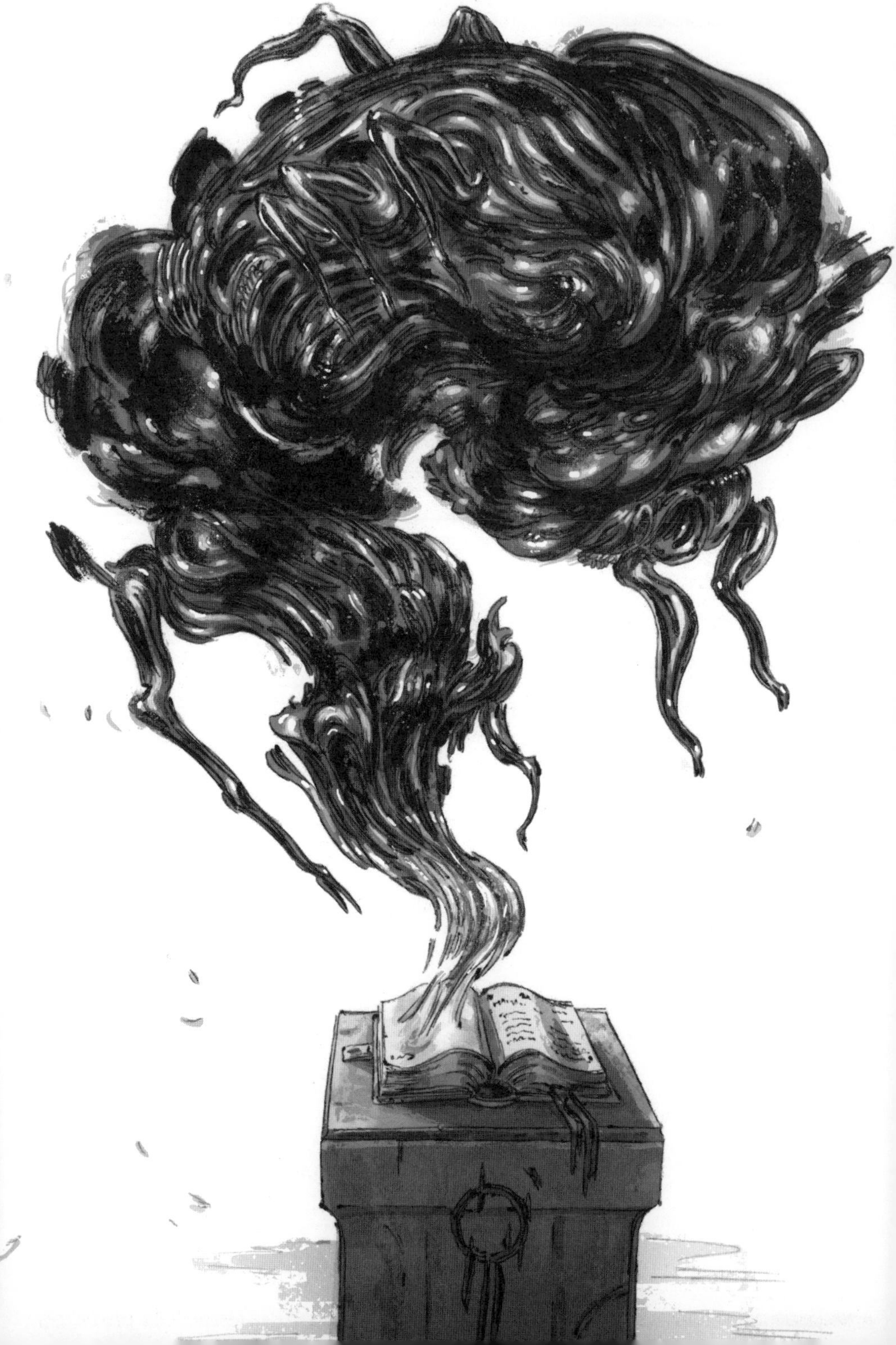

4. One of the character's facial features (each eye, nose, mouth) is overwritten and becomes useless. The mouth may be reopened by cutting through the flesh (doing 1 hit point of damage), but will look a total mess.
5. One of the character's packs (chosen at random) becomes a mere sketch line, as does everything in it, evaporating momentarily into nothing.
6. The character appears to everyone else as a black and white line drawing, although the character sees himself normally and perceives the rest of the world as black and white line drawings. The character will be able to communicate with the real world, but his ability to interact with the world becomes limited. Floors, boats, and other flattish surfaces will continue to support the character, and doors, walls, and so on will continue to obstruct the character as normal.

   Unfortunately, the character cannot physically manipulate anything within the world. Of course that also means that nothing in the world can really harm the character either, which is handy because those not accustomed and friendly to weird and magical effects will treat the character as an absolute monster.

   The only way to restore the character is to commission a master artist to paint the character back into reality. Such an artist cannot be found in Schwarzton, and in fact once found will charge 1d20x1000sp to do the work (half if a very good Reaction Roll is made).

   A lesser artist can do the work, but the character will be unrealistically ugly, appear unnatural, and lose 1d6 Constitution and Charisma points.

11. Doors

Both heavy stone doors here are locked with standard locks, but the keys have long since been lost.

12. Doors

All three heavy stone doors here are locked with standard locks, but the keys have long since been lost.

13. Catacombs

These rough narrow tunnels house the bodies of the Duvan'Ku honored dead, their bones laying open on berths lining the walls. There are remains of over 100 people here. Searching the crypts will reveal 1d100x1d10sp worth of old silver coins.

14. Catacombs

These rough narrow tunnels house the bodies of the Duvan'Ku honored dead, their bones laying open on berths lining the walls. There are remains of over 100 people here. Searching the crypts will reveal 1d100x1d10sp worth of old silver coins.

15. The Stairs

The stairs here are rather steep (60°) and a bit inconvenient, the ceiling only being six feet above the stairs. The walls and ceiling are absolutely identical for the entire length of the staircase to the point where not even a successful Architecture roll will reveal that one stretch of wall is different from another, but the fact that it is preternaturally the same all the way along their length.

16. The Endless Stairs

Once the Eye has been seen (location #17), it is impossible to return up the stairs here to the dungeon without completing the ritual described (again, location #17). Instead of turning east here, the stairs will continue on, going 80' more before turning east there. It will then continue to on top of the current set of stairs, eternally climbing. This means that anyone on the stairs at this point and beyond is no longer inside the hill as they will have climbed higher than the hill's crest. Not that this will matter to anyone on the stairs as the only thing to do on the staircase in the dark passage is climb, climb, climb.

The original turnoff at this keyed location will simply not exist. Any attempt to search for it will fail as it is not hidden by an illusion and using magic or force to go through the wall will not find the original passage leading back up to location #11. Again, it no longer exists, and will not exist until the ritual at location #17 is performed.

17. The Eye and the Basin

At the end of this hallway is a sculpture of The Eye of Many Eyes, a man-sized eyeball which is filled with smaller eye-sized eyeballs, carved directly from the wall. Nearby on the north wall is a basin, also carved from the wall, which is filled with an inky black liquid.

Inside the basin are a number of very old hearts, preserved by the liquid just enough to be recognizable. (The inky black stuff is poisonous, make a saving throw versus Poison or die if anyone is stupid enough to drink the stuff.) Inside one heart is a small gem worth 500sp.

Anyone seeing the Eye is transported to an alternate reality, one where the stairs leading up from here never end (see location #16). In order to return back to the original reality where the stairs indeed lead back to the rest of the dungeon, a fresh heart must be placed into the basin. (The party does employ retainers, yes?)

This arrangement has several consequences:

Anyone who has looked at the Eye can no longer communicate with, see, or touch anyone who has not, nor can possessions be exchanged with anyone who has not looked at the Eye. If one member of the party remains on the stairs while the rest examine the Eye and basin, there will be two consequences. The most obvious one is that the character who remains behind will not see the Eye, but if the characters who went forward to examine the Eye return up the stairs without providing a heart they will not encounter the character keeping watch, nor will that character in any way see or hear the party passing by.

Anyone not in the hallway before the eye will not return to their original reality when a heart is placed in the basin. I hope nobody was around the corner keeping watch on the stairs...

Once a fresh heart is placed in the basin, the Eye no longer has an effect on them (putting a heart into the basin then immediately looking at the Eye doesn't re-trap them) until they leave the Eye's view. If they look at the Eye after that, they are indeed trapped again (putting a heart into the basin, going around the corner and starting up the stairs, then returning and looking at the Eye does re-trap!).

18. The Door

This locked heavy stone door is carved in the shape of a ghostly face on the south side, with a lock inside its fanged, open mouth. The north side has no lock or other opening mechanism; the door must be opened from the south side.

The stone key from location #8 can be used to unlock the door, but doing so deadlocks the doors at locations #20, 22, 23, 24, and 30, so that their normal mechanisms will not open those doors. Only by locking this door with the key from the south side while the door is closed will release the deadlocks. Using other means to open the door, such as picking the lock, does not deadlock the other doors.

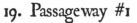

19. Passageway #1

In this corridor, whenever the door at location #18 and/or the door at location #20 are open for more than 10 seconds, the ceiling becomes strongly magnetized. All magnetic metal objects (copper, silver, and gold are not magnetic) are drawn immediately to the ceiling. Characters in magnetic metal armor will fall to the ceiling, and those carrying magnetic metal items in-hand will be hanging from the ceiling if they do not let go. Magnetic metal items inside backpacks, sacks, etc. will either drag the container (and possibly the character carrying/wearing it!) to the ceiling, or rip through it spilling the rest of its contents to the floor.

The magnetism will not stop until both doors are closed, and then it stops abruptly, everything stuck to the ceiling falling immediately.

20. The Door

This locked door is made of smooth, featureless marble. Affixed to the south face of marble is a dial with the Roman numerals I-XII around the edge. This is a combination lock, and the combination is Right-IV, Left-III, Right-I. The lock can be smashed to open the door, but then this door would be considered 'open' for the purposes of location #19 and #21's effects.

The door may be easily pushed open from the north side.

21. Passageway #2

In this corridor, whenever the door at location #20 and/or the door at location #24 are open, the room begins to heat up. For the first five rounds, the heat is merely noticeable. Then after that, anyone within the room takes 1 hit point of damage every five rounds. After twenty-five more rounds, they take one point of damage every round.

When both doors are shut, the heat dissipates immediately.

22. The Door

This locked door is made of solid steel, with four pale stones mounted on the wall – one blue, one red, one green, and one yellow. They are buttons and can be pressed with great effort, each press taking one round. When a button is pressed, it remains in the door until all of the buttons have been pressed, and then they slowly rise up again to their original positions, taking two rounds before any can again be pressed. The door will open if the buttons are pressed in the following order: red, green, blue, and yellow.

The west face of the door is smooth and has no lock or other opening mechanism; the door must be opened from the east side.

23. The Door

This locked heavy stone door is in the shape of a ghostly face on the west side, with a lock inside its fanged, open mouth. There is no mechanism for opening the door on the east side; the door must be opened from the west side.

If the incorrect key is used to open the door (and the correct key is long gone), or if any attempt to pick the lock fails, the mouth will clamp shut, automatically trapping at least one hand (the lock-fiddler must make a saving throw versus Paralyze to avoid both hands being trapped). This will not inflict damage on the character picking the lock. Instead the mouth will simply never let go.

The surface stone covering the door is brittle, so it possible to smash the stone and free anyone who has his hand held by the mouth. Unfortunately, the stone will only break off in small chunks and shards. The shards are razor sharp and will inflict 1d4 hit points of damage to anyone within 5'. A saving throw versus Breath Weapon will halve this damage, but anyone trapped by the mouth will be unable to avoid these flying shards and cannot make this saving throw. It will take 2d4 blows to free a trapped character.

24. The Door

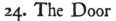

This is an airtight metal hatch with a wheel mechanism in its center used to open the door (it opens southward – very important). At present it is 'locked,' but turning the wheel is sufficient to open the door. (If the 'lock' is disabled from location #6, it becomes unable to be re-sealed). There is a wheel on both sides of the door.

25. Cell Block A

The walls to this corridor are adorned with many, many runes. Anyone looking at them must make a saving throw versus Magic or be inflicted with madness. This madness will take one of six forms (roll randomly):

1. The character simply cannot tolerate open doors. Any door must be shut or the character will stab-kill-hurt until the door is shut!
2. The character will gain an innate sense of direction and will not take one step to the west. Not one! Never never never!
3. Severe claustrophobia! The character will collapse in a ball and sob and whimper until removed to an outdoor location.
4. The character goes catatonic, aware of his surroundings, but unable to interact. He is completely unresponsive.
5. The character sees all weapons as poisonous snakes, and will make sure that there are no weapons being held or worn by anyone!
6. The character finds that anything touching the skin is absolutely unbearable! No clothing, no armor, no equipment, nothing in hand, nobody touching (or restraining!), nothing!

The effect ends when the character is outside and breathes in fresh air.

The west door is 3' thick marble, with five heavy steel bars set across it to prevent it from being opened. The bars are very heavy, but otherwise very easily removed.

26. The Cell

This cell contains the Luck Sucker, which unless measures have been taken will have detected the opening of the door at location #22 and be pressed against the door of its cell. When the cell door is opened, it will spill out into the corridor and attack!

The Luck Sucker

The creature resembles a giant bald caterpillar, perhaps 15' long. Its insides, instead of being made of fleshy stuff, consist in fact of a bright neon liqueous ooze. It feeds on ill fortune, and forces confrontations in order to facilitate incidents of bad luck.

The Luck Sucker is Armor 12, Hit Dice 8, Movement 90', 1 bite attack doing 1d6 damage plus ooze injection, Morale 12.

The Luck Sucker also has many special abilities:

- When it hits in combat, some of the creature's interior ooze is injected into the target's body unless a saving throw versus Poison is made. This ooze is a luck sponge, good for 1d6 occurrences of bad luck. Whenever a non-combat roll is called for (wandering monsters, climbing, randomly determining treasure, etc.) the worst possible result is automatically generated. When all of the bad luck is used up, the ooze solidifies within the character and takes 1d4 days to pass, during which time the character can do nothing but curl up in agony.
- Any natural 1 on an Initiative roll by foes opposing the creature gives a +1 bonus to all of the creature's future Initiative rolls.
- Any natural 1 on a to-hit roll against the creature increases its Armor rating by 1.
- Any natural 1 on a damage roll against it does no damage, but instead adds to the creature's hit points the maximum amount of damage that is possible. For instance, if it was hit with a weapon that did 1d8 damage, and the damage roll was a 1, it adds 8 hit points to its total.

It may exceed its regular maximum hit points in this manner. If an attack does multiple dice of damage, this is based on each individual die, not the total rolled.

- Due to its lack of a skeleton, it is immune to attacks by blunt weapons. It can also squeeze through small spaces. If a drop of water can pass through a space, so can the Luck Sucker.
- Any attack against it that does damage will pierce its skin, causing the interior muck to splatter the area around the wound. The attacker and anyone within 10' (assuming a mêlée attack) must make a saving throw versus Paralyze or be covered in the stuff. This substance will glow for 1d6 hours (bright enough that the character can be seen in darkness, but not bright enough to see with), and during that time all natural 2s are counted as natural 1s (assuming a 1 is bad for that particular roll).
- Once per day it can excrete a gaseous mist which covers a 50' radius area. All within must make a saving throw versus Breath Weapon (even though it comes out the opposite end!) or make all rolls with a one-step more disadvantageous die type for the next 1d4 hours. For example, to-hit rolls would not be made on a 1d20, but on a 1d12 (if a player has one of those weird 16-siders or something, let him use that instead, but only for the player that owns the die!), and skill rolls would not be made on 1d6, but on 1d8, because in both cases that adjustment makes success more difficult.

All effects are cumulative.

27. Cell Block B

The east door is a simple steel door, but the cracks between the door and the wall it is set in have been sealed with rubber. If anyone wants to open the door, the rubber will have to be torn or scraped away.

If this seal is broken, the western door (location #23) will automatically slam shut. Anyone standing in the doorway should be asked, "Inside or outside?" and make a saving throw versus Paralyze. Success means that the character takes no damage and ends up on the intended side of the door. Failure means that he suffers 1d6 hit points of damage and has an even chance to wind up on either side of the door. If the character attempts to hold the door open, or not move, then he will die as the door shuts anyway, crushing him into a goo.

The western door will not open again until the eastern door is closed and sealed in some manner.

28. The Cell

This seemingly empty, featureless cell contains a disembodied consciousness which can only possess the excrement of living beings. When the cell door is opened, the being will immediately be in the guts of every living creature present, causing severe debilitating pain as the being forces stomach acid through the intestinal tract (certain chemical properties of the acid is what allows the being to propel the resulting mass), and in two rounds all within the area will vacate their bowels.

Each combination of piss and shit, even though possessing one collective consciousness, will act independently. What they do will depend on how the individual generating the waste is dressed:

- A being that is naked, or wearing a dress or kilt or the like with no underwear, will simply take 1 hit point of damage as the waste slithers and sloshes its way down one leg to the floor, and then wobble towards the exit.
- If the being is wearing normal clothes, the waste will gather and take two rounds to eat through the cloth before plopping to the floor, causing 2 hit points of damage.
- If the being is wearing stiff clothing (the sort one wears for off-road wilderness travel), it will take three rounds, and inflict 3 hit points of damage, before the mess is free.

- If the being is wearing chain armor pants or something equally ridiculous, it will take four rounds, and inflict 4 hit points of damage, before draining out through the holes in the armor.
- Any character wearing plate armor or equivalent will find himself in trouble as the slop trickles down his legs and becomes trapped within his armor. This will do 1 hit point of damage every round until the character can strip off the armor (1d6 rounds if cutting all the buckles and straps, 1d10+10 rounds if taking it off 'properly,' piece by piece).

Once a mass of excreta is free, it has the following stats: Armor 12, Hit Dice 1, Movement 30', 1 touch attack doing 1 hit point of acid damage, Morale 4. It is immune to physical attacks (why would bashing, cutting, or stabbing poo hurt it?), causing it at worst to separate into smaller independent units. It must be frozen, burned, or contained in glass – and that means every last drop.

Whenever any bit of any mass of this psychic excreta comes within 50' of another living creature, it will also invade and vacate the bowels of that creature.

Remember that once one character or creature has been cleared out, the body will always produce more! Every six turns the body will generate enough waste for the creature to take it over again.

29. Passageway #3

Holes, each about 6" in diameter, cover the walls of this passageway. These holes slope downward, the tubes extending down for over a mile before reaching advanced technology pumping mechanisms and holding tanks.

In the middle of the hallway is a portcullis with a closed, but not locked, gate in its center. The latch for the gate has three handles: two are red, one is blue. If this gate is opened using the first red handle or the blue handle, then the air is sucked out through the holes, subjecting the room to explosive decompression. The players should be informed that the air is violently being sucked out of their characters' lungs; their reaction will be important. The vacuum produces several ill effects:

- All characters must make a saving throw versus Paralyze, or suffer permanent -1 adjustments to their Constitution modifiers (the modifier, not the base score). If a character tries to hold his breath as the air is sucked from the room, his lungs rupture: he automatically fails this save and must make another to avoid suffering another -1 Constitution modifier penalty, plus he will take 2d6 hit points of damage.
- All flames will be immediately extinguished and cannot be relit.
- All items will be sucked towards the holes, and characters must make a saving throw versus Paralyze for every item they are holding or that is being loosely stashed in a pack or case or scabbard. Failure means these items are sucked down a hole (or at least slam into the wall if they are not big enough to fit in the holes). The explosive decompression lasts less than a second in such a confined area so anything that cannot immediately be sucked through the holes, will not be. People will be momentarily jerked towards the walls, but will not be slammed into them. (Well, to be fun, if anyone looking directly into a hole when the decompression happens must make a saving throw versus Paralyze or have his eyes sucked out of his head.)
- Any sealed containers burst open, including all vials containing potions.
- Spells can still be cast as the vacuum is not quite perfect. Sound cannot travel enough for anyone to ever hear it, but enough that spells will work. However, because the caster cannot hear what he is doing, he must make a saving throw versus Magic to correctly cast the spell.
- Characters lose 1 hit point of damage per round because of the lack of air.
- The doors to the north and south (locations #24 and #30) will absolutely not open, having been pulled shut by the loss of pressure in this room.

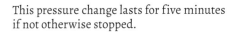

This pressure change lasts for five minutes if not otherwise stopped.

30. The Door

This is an airtight metal hatch with a wheel mechanism in its center used to open the door (it opens northward – very important). The center of the wheel has an impression of a (right) human hand, with a reversed Dead Sign in the center, seemingly melted into it. Although no heat seems to emanate from the wheel, placing a hand into this impression will burn the hand to the point where skin will stick to the wheel when the hand is pulled back. The hand will have a Dead Sign permanent seared into the hand which no Clerical magic can remove. This does no damage, but the hand will be useless for 1d4 days. Placing a hand in the impression also stops the vacuum effect in location #29, with air returning to the room.

At present the door is 'locked,' but turning the wheel is sufficient to open the door. (If the 'lock' is disabled from location #6, it becomes unable to be re-sealed). There is a wheel on both sides of the door, but only the wheel on the south side has the hand impression. The door's surface, including the wheel, is coated in copper on the north side.

31. The Dragon Altar

This room has two mummified dragon heads with their mouths open mounted on both the east and west wall. It is obvious that a similar mummified dragon head was once mounted on the north wall, but all that now remains is the stump of a neck out of which trickles the slightest stream of acidic liquid.

Before this neck is an altar, plain but for the Dead Sign carved into the sides. On the altar is a fabulous golden goblet inlaid with gems. It is empty, but bloodstained. The goblet is worth 3000sp.

So what happens if the goblet is grabbed?

- If neither the treasures nor the bodies in locations #13 or #14 have been disturbed, then the goblet may be taken. No problem!
- If even one silver piece was taken from the catacombs, and the goblet is so much as touched, the headless dragon's stump will spew acid with volcanic force. Anyone within reach of the goblet or in a straight line to the south, will suffer 3d12 hit points of damage (make a saving throw versus Breath Weapon for half damage) from the acid, and any equipment not made from precious metals or gemstones will melt! If the door is shut, this acid will splash around so everyone else in the room suffers 1d12 hit points of damage (make a saving throw versus Breath Weapon for half damage). If the door is open, the acid will destroy the next three doors (up to and including location #20!), which will trigger the explosive decompression, which will slam the location #30 door shut.
- If any of the corpses in the catacombs were damaged, or if there is any effort to damage any of the dragon heads here, then the heads on the east and west walls will breathe dragonfire, and the severed head will spew its acid. The acid and dragonfire forms an explosive combination which will blow out all the doors down to locations #11 and #12!

  While the conflagration will blow out the doors at locations #22 and #23, the doors to the cells at locations #26 and #28 will remain intact. Anyone in that entire area will take 10d12 hit points of damage (make a saving throw versus Breath Weapon for half damage) and anything even arguably flammable will burn to ashes and the acid will melt the ashes as well as anything that was not flammable. Precious metals and gems will not be spared this time.

Note that there is no mechanical means connecting the goblet and the dragon heads, so searching for traps cannot reveal that anything will happen if the goblet is moved.

The Meteor Strike

This is the location where the 'meteor' struck, leaving a massive crater and a one foot diameter chunk of rock split directly in half.

The 'meteor' looks like a rock on the outside, but on the inside is lined with charred bits of worked metal and metal thread, and basically looks like someone blew up a fancy clock.

The Satanic Coven & Their Cave

There is indeed a 'Satanic' coven operating out of Schwarzton, but it is not very threatening. It consists of a group of men, all seemingly happily married with children, who have come into contact with a strange alien creature. They should be fairly 'invisible' during the party's initial investigation in the village, simply because they have nothing to do with the missing children. They fear, along with the rest of their fellows, that someone is up in the Old Haunted Hill causing this trouble, so if any of them are encouraging the player characters to investigate it, they mean it, they genuinely mean it and for two reasons. First because they are truly concerned about the well-being of their fellow villagers and want any threat removed, and second, because if this other cult is eliminated, they no longer have to be afraid of being found out and then punished for taking their neighbors' children.

Once the characters have been to the Old Haunted Hill and returned to Schwarzton to inform the villagers that their children are not there, the actual 'Satanists' will become spooked. One will be there when the report is made, and he will be visibly shaken before suspiciously excusing himself and heading straight for the coven's 'temple' — a cave in the hills. Following him will be no problem since he is so distracted, and if confronted and threatened with any credible consequences, will tell the party where the cave is.

That cave is the place where the coven gathers to please and to be rewarded by their master. It is a fair walk away from the village, but not so far that members of the Satanic Coven cannot get there and back in a fairly short amount of time.

If the player characters follow one of the members of the coven to the cave, they will come across a scene of complete oddity. There are over half a dozen men in the cave, some wearing the skins of the missing animals as capes or scarves (if the animal is small) and the heads of the animals as masks. Otherwise naked, the men are engaging in a homosexual orgy on a stone floor absolutely saturated with animal blood and guts while grunting and panting words as if they were having sex with women. Meanwhile, a walking penis staggers around between the participants of the orgy slurping up the blood and guts that is all over the place.

Awkward.

When this lot notices the player characters, they will be very pleased to see them. The men will think that more women are showing up. The walking penis will be pleased to see them because maybe they have got some sense and can actually help it... which just might cause the player characters to end up seeing the members of the coven as being quite attractive and willing and boy isn't it getting warm in here...

The bottom line is that these 'cultists' are absolutely harmless. The animals that went missing were taken by their owners to both feed their 'master' and to have something 'appropriate' to wear at the orgies. Yes, they shout "Hail Satan!" (of course they do, who else would appear as a goat penis and help them get laid?) and fornicate and commit adultery, but they are just being naughty, not evil. None of them would ever be aggressive towards anyone, let alone a child. They have got nothing to do with the disappearances of the children, and in fact stopped taking animals after the children began to go missing out of fear that they would be discovered and then blamed for the children.

If things get to the point where the aphrodisiac effect wears off, all of these guys will pretend to be completely oblivious to what has been going on ("Hey, where'd the girls go?") except for one of them who will just get this really big grin on his face. They have clothing and basic wilderness equipment (hatchet, dagger, etc.) so if they could reach them they could defend themselves if attacked, but they will not want to actually fight unless the player characters are absolute psychos determined to kill them. Doubtless the Referee can sympathize, knowing as well as I do that going into combat naked just after sex (and perhaps interrupted sex!) is not high on the list of anyone's priorities. The cultists' main motivations will be first, to keep their activities secret from the others in Schwarzton – specifically their wives, and second, to weasel their way into still coming up here and 'worshipping Satan.'

That walking penis has motivations of its own...

The Penis Walker

The penis walker is an eight inch long telepathic alien whose ship recently crashed nearby. Naked, lost, and cut off from all communication, it did what it had to do to survive – hunted for food and clothing (killed a goat, ate its flesh, made a coat for itself) and found shelter (the cave).

It is a powerful telepath and empath, but unfortunately its brain lengths are not entirely compatible with human brain lengths, resulting in miscommunication, especially with less intelligent and less sensitive humans. It wanted friendship and assistance gaining food, the contacted villagers took that to mean worship and sacrifice. It tried to send out warm feelings to communicate friendship, instead it inflamed the primitive humans' libidos.

The walker itself is Armor 12, Hit Dice 0, Movement 30', and Morale 2. It has no attacks that do physical damage (the retractable filaments in its head paralyze much like a jellyfish's stingers, but are wholly ineffective against creatures bigger than 50 pounds or so), but its telepathic abilities are impressive:

- It can communicate telepathically with beings that are intelligent enough. Those who are less intelligent will receive a garbled message. For example, the following is what the creature will mentally 'say' to those who first come across it in its cave, surrounded by the 'worshippers,' as determined by each character's combined Intelligence and Wisdom:
  - 14 or less: "Kill! Kill! Must Feed! Kill! Kill!"
  - 15-17: "Bring me animals! Kill animals for me! I will bestow favor to you if you bring animals and kill them for me!"
  - 18-29: "Please, I am lost and hungry. Feed me, please! I require fresh meat for sustenance!"
  - 30 or more: "Greetings, Earthlings! I am Nrrrgxt'ststlo of Antares 6. My vessel was damaged and crashed nearby. These poor deluded fellows cannot understand me

properly, but I mean no harm. I merely require feed animals for sustenance. Do you know of a remote repair facility in this star system? Or a communications uplink? My transmitter was destroyed and I fear I'm creating something of a ruckus just by being here. I so hate being a bother."

- It can detect feelings and thoughts directly concerning itself. This ability has no range limit, so it can detect its children back on Antares 6 missing their parent (and they can detect that it wants to return to them), it can feel its mate's annoyance at the long absence which leads to pleasure coupling with another (and the mate can feel this one's feelings of betrayal and jealousy and desperation, and takes satisfaction in that), it detects the 'cultists' feelings of worship and feeling naughty for being all 'Satanic,' and it will know with 100% certainty how any of the player characters feel towards it, if they tell others about it (because it will then detect those others' thoughts), etc.
- It can read the emotions and thoughts of everyone in the immediate vicinity, and can decide to become immersed in them if it so desires. (For this reason it enjoys the 'Satanic Orgies' it inspires, as humans feeling good makes it feel good, and what feels better than an orgy?)
- It releases its feelings like a mental cloud to be breathed in by anyone nearby, and it does this unconsciously and cannot turn it off. Humans (and near-humans) do not deal very well with this, and must make saving throws versus Poison or receive the message very strangely:
  - Expressing happiness and friendship is received by the human body as an aphrodisiac. The character becomes strongly aroused, and every member of the same species appears to the character as a beautiful specimen of the character's preferred sexual preference.
  - Expressing surprise or panic or fear is received by the human body as an active threat, and it will appear as though those nearby are attacking.
  - Expressing sadness or regret will be received by the human body as if the air itself is burning, and the character will scream and flail about wildly.
  - Actual anger will cause blinding pain, requiring a saving throw to make any action (move, attack, speak, etc.)

The Bear

The 'Satanic Cult' was actually a group of morons sacrificing their own animals believing they were getting to sin under the protection of a great dark power. They were never going to hurt anyone.

Nobody from the village has been up to the Great Haunted Hill in ages, so the children didn't go there.

So what did happen to them?

The bear.

A gigantic brown bear has wandered far from its usual territory high in the mountains, and was the first Earth creature encountered by the crash-landed alien. Its attempts at telepathic communication with the bear awakened a more advanced, albeit still bear-filtered, intelligence. It has become a sly hunter, taking defenseless children wandering on their own while avoiding more dangerous adults and doing a decent job of covering its own tracks, but its mental condition is deteriorating, as a bear's brain was not built to support this sort of thought, and it will not remain hidden forever.

There is a cumulative 1 in 10 chance per day spent wandering around the countryside (including moving to and from the Old Haunted Hill or the Satanic cave) that the bear will be encountered.

The Bear: Armor 14, Hit Dice 6, Movement 150', 1 maul attack doing 1d8 damage, if to-hit roll succeeds by 5 or more (or if a natural 20 is rolled), damage is on-going each round as the bear grabs hold of its target in a deadly hug, Morale 9.

Greetings Intrepid Adventurers!

I trust you are doing well and your current quest is going most splendidly. Would you like a little gift that would enhance your chances of success for the future? Of course you do!

The volume of knowledge here, Charting the Heavens, may seem like a boring, if accurate, summation of current astronomical knowledge. I happen to know that it is an acrostic, where the first letters of every section impart their own wisdom. Do go through and pay attention to that, you'll be most pleased I assure you.

I leave this gift for you as a gesture of goodwill. I may need the assistance of a hearty group of high-minded adventurers myself one of these days. I certainly get up to more mischief than any one man can responsibly handle, so it's best to make friends when one can. So enjoy the gift, and remember who it was that gave it to you. With luck the only favor you need do in return is paying the tab for a round of drinks when we finally meet, but one never knows what life will rain down on one's head, especially those of us who go to places named things like The Old Haunted Hill. Sometimes I think we're all mad, living this life.

Oh, and I must tell you that you're barking up the wrong tree with this silly hill though. It's got nothing to do with what you're trying to do right now. I'd suggest skipping it entirely and doing more investigation within the village, as all that you'll find within the cave is danger and treasure. I suppose I've just guaranteed that you'll go in there, but really, it's got nothing to do with the missing kids.

Still if you do want to explore, keep in mind that inside the cave there are three different secret passages. And if you come across the three levers, do not, whatever you do, push all three levers down. It won't reveal

a super-secret hidden treasure or anything. And you'll need a strong heart to survive all of the challenges in that place.

Always your friend,

Iri-Khan

Master of the Mystic Arts

LAMENTATIONS *of the* FLAME PRINCESS

ADVENTURES

DEATH LOVE DOOM

LAMENTATIONS *of the* FLAME PRINCESS ADVENTURES

DEATH LOVE DOOM

Written by James Edward Raggi IV

Edited by Matthew Pook

Illustrated by Kelvin Green

Cover Design, Cartography and Graphic Design by Jez Gordon

The Dead Sign Designed by Laura Jalo

First Printed in 2012

CONTENTS

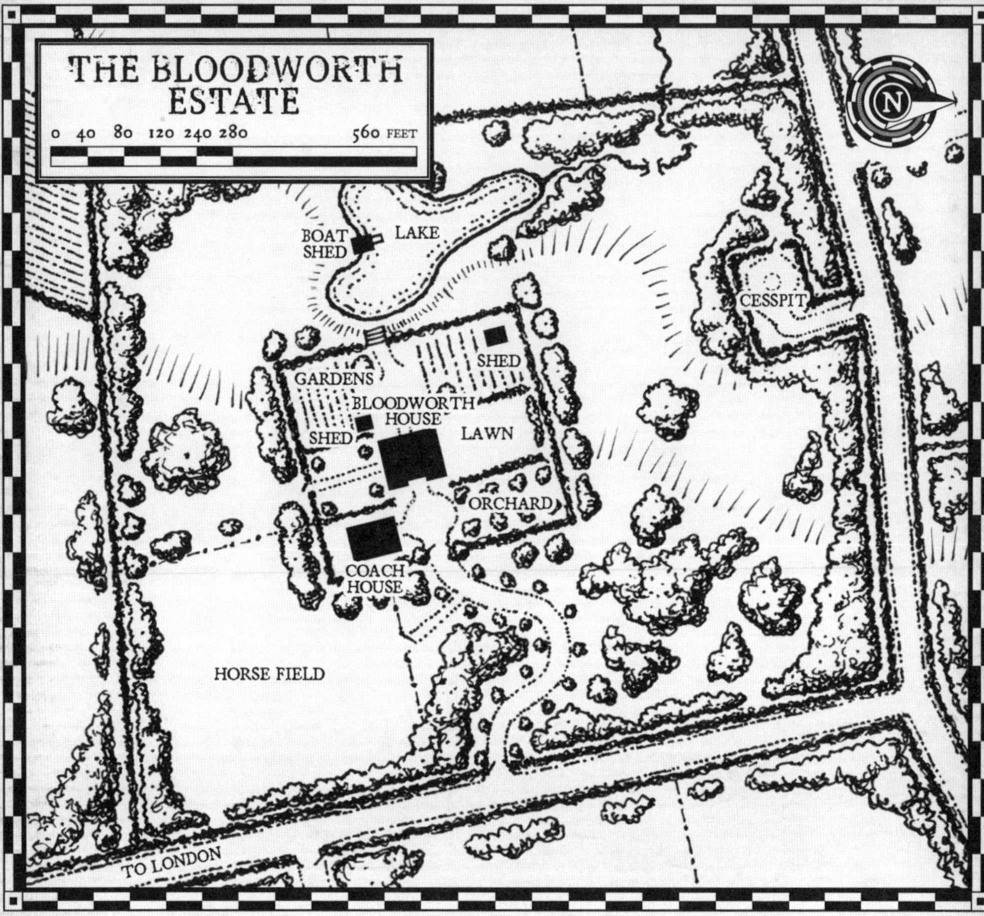
THE BLOODWORTH ESTATE
0 40 80 120 240 280 560 FEET
N
BOAT SHED
LAKE
CESSPIT
SHED
GARDENS
BLOODWORTH HOUSE
SHED
LAWN
ORCHARD
COACH HOUSE
HORSE FIELD
TO LONDON

THE COACH HOUSE

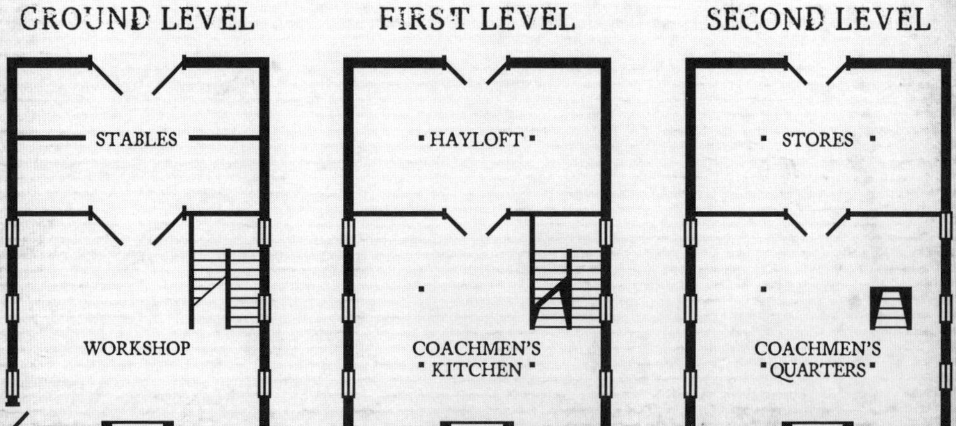
GROUND LEVEL
FIRST LEVEL
SECOND LEVEL
STABLES
WORKSHOP
HAYLOFT
COACHMEN'S KITCHEN
STORES
COACHMEN'S QUARTERS

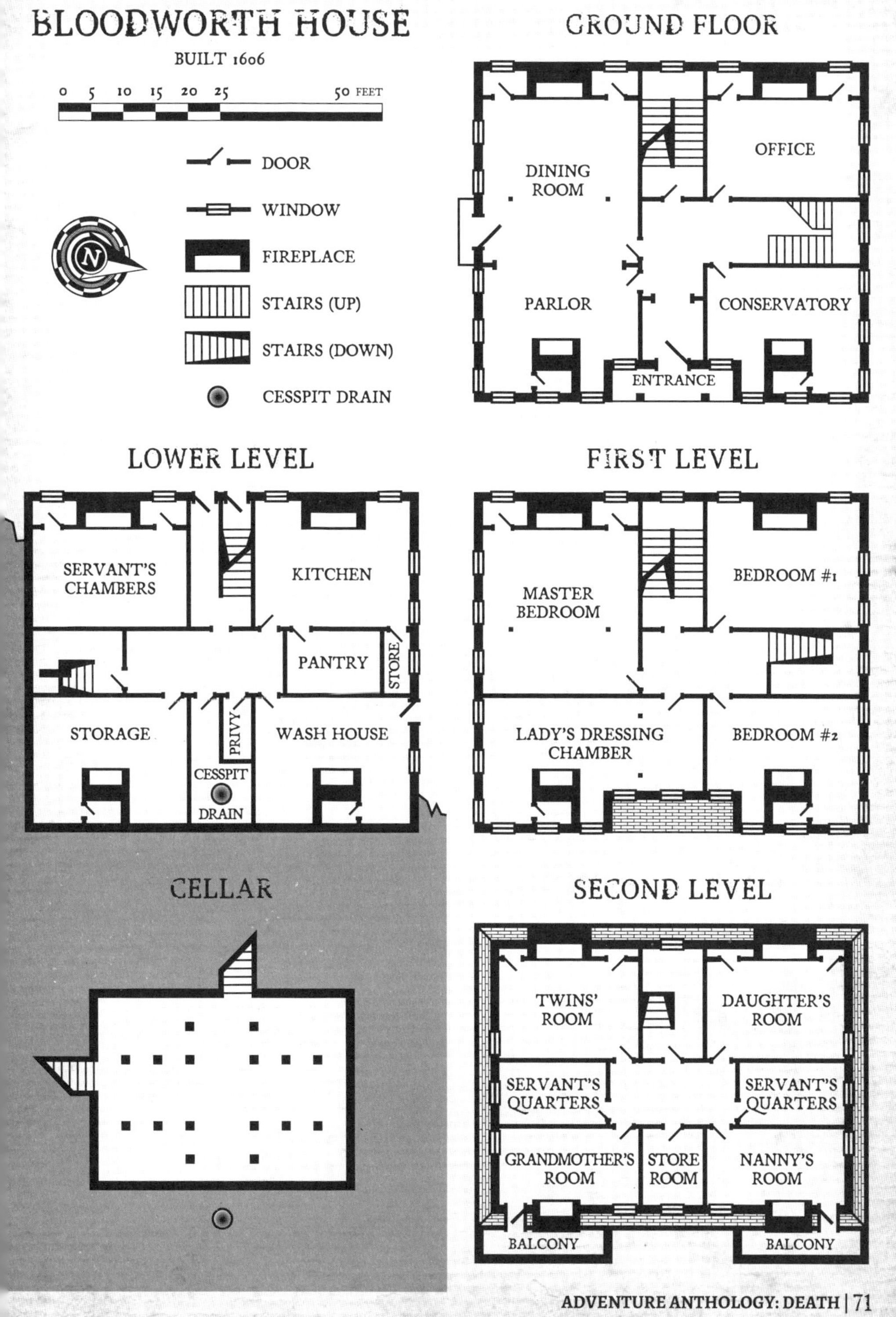
BLOODWORTH HOUSE
BUILT 1606
0 5 10 15 20 25 50 FEET
DOOR
WINDOW
FIREPLACE
STAIRS (UP)
STAIRS (DOWN)
CESSPIT DRAIN
N
GROUND FLOOR
DINING ROOM
OFFICE
PARLOR
CONSERVATORY
ENTRANCE
LOWER LEVEL
SERVANT'S CHAMBERS
KITCHEN
PANTRY
STORE
STORAGE
PRIVY
WASH HOUSE
CESSPIT DRAIN
FIRST LEVEL
MASTER BEDROOM
BEDROOM #1
LADY'S DRESSING CHAMBER
BEDROOM #2
CELLAR
SECOND LEVEL
TWINS' ROOM
DAUGHTER'S ROOM
SERVANT'S QUARTERS
SERVANT'S QUARTERS
GRANDMOTHER'S ROOM
STORE ROOM
NANNY'S ROOM
BALCONY
BALCONY

Author's Notes

I was originally going to have this introduction be about "extreme" media and blah blah about creative freedom, because this adventure was originally conceived as a "blood and guts and pussies and cocks and dismembered children" exercise in silliness. But then I actually started caring about the meat of the adventure and something different came out the other end.

My first marriage was a complete mess as lives on totally different tracks intersected at just the right/ wrong time. I ended up living across the world, a situation that was honestly more about escaping a life I hated than anything else. Finland was the right place, but unfortunately, the person I was with wasn't quite right.

The actual end of a marriage isn't the horrible part. It's the most painful, as you are forced to march forward into a new life because there is no going back. No status quo to give even a moment's comfort. That really sucks, but generally people are better off being not with the wrong person. As I'm looking out of my Helsinki window right now while performing my job as a full-time RPG writer and publisher, my ex is up north and expecting her second child. Neither of these things would be possible if we'd stayed together.

The horrible part is the lead-up to the break. The knowledge that everything is wrong and nothing is working, but you made this promise and you can't help how you feel and why doesn't the other person understand what they're doing to us?

It's lonelier than actually being alone. Then someone catches your eye, and you stay away from them to keep out of trouble, but an imagination so used to creating entire new worlds then starts working to manufacturing personalities, possibilities, and dare I say mythologies about someone you dare not even talk to... and then one day the person you're supposed to be spending the rest of your life with says or does that one last thing that makes you realize that there is no fixing this.

You realize you're in hell and no matter what you do, you're going to have to go through an even worse hell before anything seems right again. And pull a few people through that hell with you, because it's not like you're thinking very clearly as you decide that things just cannot continue as they are. Blow that bridge up before your confidence falters and you might be tempted to go back...

So of course, being the sensitive and mature gentleman that I am, I figure that kind of emotional mess completely justifies the blood and guts and pussies and cocks and dismembered children.

It's a metaphor, see?

That's how horror works in make-believe. Take real world pain and fear, and add fantasy bullshit. Use your life's pain to make some gaming fun. Isolating past trauma and treating it as something to mention only with the greatest reverence gives it far more importance in life than it should have. What better way to show dominance over one's painful past than to present it to others for purposes of amusement?

I'd say "Enjoy the adventure!", but maybe that's the wrong phrase to use. "I hope you find the adventure satisfying and effective," might be better. Either way, if you dare to run this for your players, drop me a line at lotfp@lotfp.com and let me know how it goes.

James Edward Raggi IV
July 8, 2012
Right Behind You

Running the Adventure

Death Love Doom is, first and foremost, a haunted house story. Its purpose is to spook the characters and players alike. The exploration and challenge aspects of the adventure, while present, are not so important.

The adventure presents two primary methods of provoking the desired reactions: The descriptions of the victims, and the grotesque nature of the wandering hostile entities. The Referee should be familiar with these, and prepared to present them in the most unsettling ways possible.

For example, describing the nature of the victims' injuries, or alterations, should be done dispassionately. It is common, in other adventures, for characters to come across the results of battle. Nobody gets excited or acts like something horrible has happened when they find a body that has been slain in normal combat. Nevermind the fact that those victims have been hacked or stabbed or smashed to death. But those scenes are often described matter-of-factly and might be everyday occurrences in a campaign. Thus the bodies in this adventure should be described the same way. No matter how unusual or disgusting the state of the victim, treat it as if it is part of the normal scenery. This will unnerve the players when they realize what they are hearing.

However, when the characters come across a live victim on the grounds, it is time to cut loose. The agony and the hopelessness must come through. People who did nothing wrong have been altered and there is nothing that anyone can really do to save them. This is what the player characters have walked into for the sake of a few coins, so really hammer them with it.

Do not let up. These are descriptions of things that the characters did not do and were not responsible for, they are not being done to the player characters, and they are simply not possible in real life. There is a separation between this fiction and real-life that cannot be confused. If players are truly uncomfortable with what is going on in the scenario, then their characters should leave the area.

Do be aware of players' limits when they encounter Grandma though, as at that point they become active participants, or more accurately the victims, of a potentially horrific situation due to her abilities.

Yet for this adventure to come alive, it must be more than an exercise in describing supernatural mutilation. The Referee must go beyond what is written here to get under the skin of the players.

From the moment that the characters enter the property, the tension must be cranked up and the proper atmosphere maintained. Even if the players are cracking jokes, going off topic, and acting like this is just another adventure, the Referee should not join in their mirth. He should remain solemn. In essence, he must put a damper on their gaiety. What has happened here is a tragedy and should be presented that way, and not as some sort of wet horror comedy a la early Peter Jackson. If players want to have that sort of fun they should be sorely disappointed at The Bloodworth House.

All of the old scary movie tricks will work. The house should be described in ominous terms. The interior of the house should be dark with menace seemingly found in every shadow. Make the weather stormy or blustery so that shutters can slam against the side of the house. Have rats skittering here and there. Anything that keeps the player characters on their toes.

And there are four moving characters on the property, and these should appear as best suits the situation. If the players have not yet found anything that spooks them, the first encounter should be sudden and surprising. Once the players are nervous, then you can have these entities make noise going through doors, using the stairs, knocking on the front door, and all the fun things that will make characters cower in fear.

Or to put it bluntly: Do everything that you can to make the characters feel threatened and the players uncomfortable while participating in this adventure. They should be constantly second-guessing their decision to be on this property and after finding even the smallest bit of loot should be discussing amongst themselves whether it is enough, whether they should leave right now.

The Setup

The bulk of the adventure takes place within the confines of a wealthy merchant's estate outside of London in the year 1625. The adventure does not have to be set outside London specifically as the city is just used for flavor; the point is that it is a large property outside of a major port city. That said, placing the adventure in London does add a certain danger to a major political event occurring in 1625.

The player characters will learn of the merchant and his property early on in the adventure (see Starting the Adventure) and then hopefully be inspired to investigate.

Certain members of the Foxlowe family (Erasmus, Penelope, Sabrina, and Myrna; for their details see the Foxlowe Family: p84) will be mobile throughout the adventure. Before play begins, the Referee must determine where these characters will be found when the player characters arrive at the property. It is best if the players do not realize that this placement is random; everything should seem to be very deliberate, if at all possible.

Roll on the following table for each of them to determine where they are before starting the adventure. Myrna and Penelope will always be found alone; it is possible for Erasmus and Sabrina to start in the same place.

1. Cellar
2. Lower Level, Servant's Chambers
3. Lower Level, Storage
4. Lower Level, Cesspit Drain
5. Lower Level, Kitchen
6. Lower Level, Pantry
7. Lower Level, Wash House
8. Ground Floor, Dining Room
9. Ground Floor, Office
10. Ground Floor, Parlor
11. Ground Floor, Conservatory
12. First Floor, Master Bedroom
13. First Floor, Bedroom #1
14. First Floor, Eldest Son's Room
15. First Floor, Dressing Chamber
16. Second Floor, Twins' Room
17. Second Level, Daughter's Room
18. Second Floor, Servants' Quarters #1
19. Second Floor, Servants' Quarters #2
20. Second Floor, Grandmother's Room
21. Second Floor, Nanny's Room
22. Outside: Submerged in the Lake
23. Outside: Orchard
24. Outside: Cesspit
25. Outside: The Garden
26. Outside: Horse Field
27. Northeast field (night only)
28. Southwest field (night only)
29. Stables Ground Floor
30. Stables First Floor

The locations of the rest of their family, the help, and any would-be robbers are noted in the location descriptions.

Starting the Adventure

Erasmus Sylvester Foxlowe is a rather successful London merchant, importing valuable items from overseas. It is a harrowing job, as investing in long-distance shipping is quite risky, and dealing with customs agents in a volatile political environment leaves one vulnerable to all sorts of accusations. But he manages, and manages well.

He does feel guilty though, as he spends most of his time in London proper while his family resides outside of town. To make up a bit for it, he often sets aside particularly lovely items his business procures as gifts for his young wife. This is especially important now that she is pregnant—with the family's fifth child!

But the latest trinket to catch his eye, part of a shipment from the Levant, is not what it seems. It is the Necklace of the Sleepless Queen, and when he returned home and gave this to his wife, Erasmus destroyed his family.

Several days have passed. The underclass that work and live around the Foxlowe offices notice that Erasmus has not returned as promised. There is talk... has something happened? Might the rich man's house outside of town be ripe for a good burglary? The word has spread, and thieves will descend upon the merchant's house the next day. Anyone hoping to beat them there had better go tonight.

To determine what the characters learn of all this, roll on the following table for every 5sp that they spend for drinks and tips to the landlord. Make a Reaction Roll, with a positive result gaining an extra roll, a negative result gaining one less.

1. Erasmus Foxlowe is a significant holder in the East India, Levant, and Virginia Companies. He specializes in precious metal and jewelry. "He's filthy stinkin' rich!"
2. Foxlowe lives outside London on an estate known as The Bloodworth House with his wife, mother, and four children.
3. Several days ago, one of Foxlowe's ships returned laden with goods. Foxlowe hasn't been heard from since receiving the vessel and returning home.
4. "Some guys I know, Eerie Frank and his fellers, they was casin' the Foxlowe place. Nothing! Not a peep! No movement! Not him, his brats, or anything! 'Looks abandoned' he says. But there hasn't been enough time to organize a proper move, so most of his stuff must still be there!"
5. "The gang is planning on hitting the house tomorrow night to see what there is to get."
6. Foxlowe has been pilfering the choicest items from his business to bring home to his wife."
7. "Have you seen that woman he has taking care of his kids? Phwoar! Can't believe his missus allows that to live under the same roof!"
8. Foxlowe lives in a proper merchant's estate and in a four story house here in town! "I ain't got four rooms, what gives 'im the right?"
9. "Foxlowe's wife is very pregnant, they surely wouldn't be traveling. Where is everyone then?"
10. "Careful when fencing anything you get from the Foxlowes. Last person to rob him was found strung up on the docks. A man like him is properly connected."
11. "Foxlowe's mother, a real piece of work from up North, is always involved with some social campaign or another, trying to take away any joy a man has. She's worse than the Puritans!"
12. "That Foxlowe don't keep no guards! Confident in His Majesty's protection, he is, but talk about just asking for it!"

If the characters want to join the gang robbing the place the following night, assume the gang is made up of d4 0 level men and d4 1 level Specialists with points in Stealth and Tinkering.

If the player characters ignore the fact that others will be hitting the property to rob it, the day following the robbery, they will learn that the robbers never returned. The next day they will hear that their friends are worried because they obviously did not score big enough to skip town; their belongings (and families, in some cases) were left behind. And Foxlowe still has not been seen back in town; "...did he take his family abroad or something?"

Once the characters arrive at The Bloodworth House, the Referee should describe their approach on the road from London, and the players will then need to decide how to proceed...

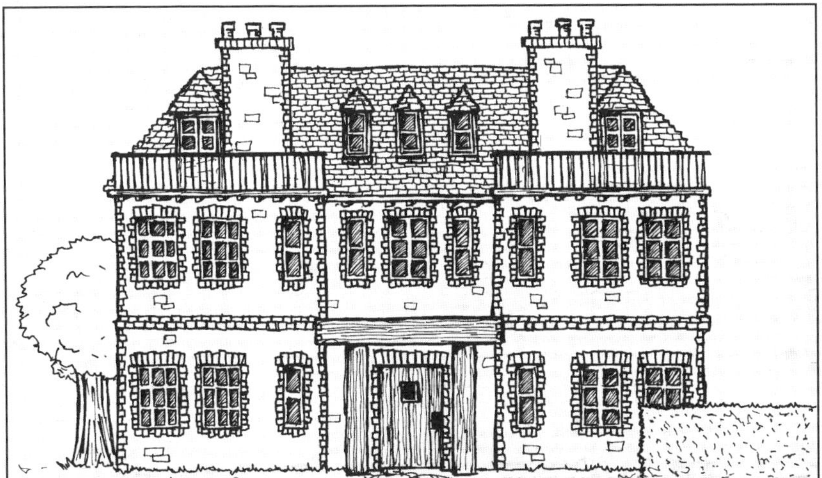

The Bloodworth Estate

Foxlowe's property, known as the Bloodworth House, is a half-hour's brisk walk from central London, close enough so that going to and from the office and the harbor and the Customs Office is not too much of a bother, but far enough away that his family can live in privacy and peace.

Boathouse

The boathouse has berths for two rowboats, but only one is present. Various maintenance gear and extra oars are also found here.

Cesspit

This entire area smells of shit and oil, and many empty casks (taken from the cellar) are strewn about the place. If a sufficient number of victims have not arrived after the tenth day of the Thing emerging from the Necklace, this will be lit, and the resulting fireball will be seen from London.

If robbers have gotten here before the player characters, one of their bodies will be floating in the cesspool, his arms, legs and head severed.

Gardens

This area is Penelope's pride and joy, and other than cutting the grass she does not allow any of the estate's servants or other members of the family to tend to it. The vegetable garden looks perfectly healthy, but pulling up any of the crop here (mainly turnips and cabbage) will reveal that they have gone sickly and twisted. If anyone takes a bite out of these malformed vegetables, they will discover that they are poisonous.

The gardens west of the house have an assortment of animal topiary (elephant, horse, squirrel, and fish). Inside the elephant topiary is the groundskeeper Samuel Longfellow, shredded up as if he had been eaten by the elephant.

These animals will sway ominously in the wind; they seem alive. Any sort of detection for magic or life will confirm that they are alive... but they will not actually move from their places or attack. They need about a month's more exposure to the energies of Duvan'Ku to be capable of that. Grandma killed the groundskeeper and placed him in her prized 'phump. The garden sheds contain mundane landscaping supplies and tools.

Lake

One of the boats from the boathouse is floating in the middle of the pond. Inside is the corpse of one of the maids, Tabitha Hammond, half-melted and covered with black sticky goo.

The Coach House

Ground Floor

Stables

The body of the stablehand and general handyman, Charles Knowles, is here, crushed under the corpse of a horse. When the horror started in the main house, the horses started to panic. This one became violent, and Knowles grabbed a pitchfork to defend himself. The horse brained Knowles with a kick, but on its way down the animal became impaled on the pitchfork. Grandma Penelope then came along and decided that this was not enough... and so sewed the two together at the crotch and lower abdomen.

There is another body of a horse here, but its head has been removed and replaced with that of the other stablehand, and coach driver, Stanley Hobart.

The coach holds four people inside the carriage, plus drivers and whoever wants to sit on the luggage area topside. The wheels of the carriage, and all the spare wheels in the coach house, have been smashed.

Workshop

This is a fully stocked workroom, equipped to take on various carpentry, metalworking, and stonework projects. All of the crates for Foxlowe's shipping business are made here, and whenever the family buys a new coach, it is customized here. Very fashionable, that.

First Floor

This was Hobart and Knowles' living and social space, serving as a kitchen, sitting room, and even a sleeping area for when one of the men sneaked female company upstairs (the Foxlowes would fire any member of their staff that they discovered to be engaged in such sinful behavior).

The east portion of the floor serves as the hayloft, and the pair were fastidious about keeping the hay out of their living quarters.

Second Floor

The loft served as the sleeping space for Charles Knowles, the Foxlowes' stablehand and handyman, and Stanley Hobart, their coachman and other stablehand. For several years, these two men were mercenaries, fighting with the Dutch in their revolt against Spain, and they even saw some action during the Bohemian Revolt. After the Battle of White Mountain in 1620, they were taken prisoner, but were later released after swearing that they would return to England and never take up arms on the Continent again.

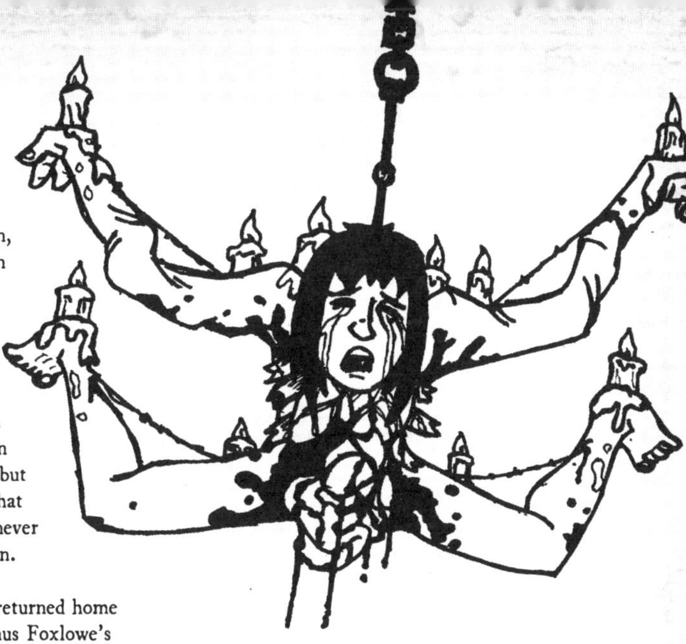

Taking their oaths seriously, they returned home and quickly found work with Erasmus Foxlowe's company. Their reticence to travel overseas for their duties and high levels of competence led Erasmus to offer them positions in his household, and they work as groundskeepers, grooms, coach drivers, and if necessary, bodyguards.

They have an assortment of weapons here, all in fine working order. They each have an arquebus and all of the requisite equipment for it, a supply of shot and powder, swords, daggers, and a suit of pikeman's armor each. Each has his own cash stash—Knowles' is 639sp and Hobart's is 1821sp.

Stanley Hobart's body is here in his bed, his head missing and a horse's head sewn on in its place.

Bloodworth House

The windows of the house are obscured by various things: The lower level windows have been stained by smoke, the curtains have been drawn on the ground and first levels, and the second level windows seem curiously reflective.

All of the rooms will have the expected furnishings in them. Bedrooms will have beds, the parlor chairs, etc. Everything in the house will be of a quality reflecting the Foxlowes' wealth and standing, with the possible exception of furnishings (and certainly personal effects) in the servants' quarters.

Ground Floor

Anyone on this floor will hear sobs coming from the direction of the dining room.

Conservatory

The family's music room contains a harpsichord, and in the storeroom behind the fireplace, several violins.

Stuffed up in the chimney in the fireplace is the body of one of the maids, Eleanor Smittsby. She has been crushed into the shape of a ball the original size of her head, placed up there, and then expanded back out to fill the space.

Three small statues (worth 250sp apiece) are on display here.

Dining Room

This is where Erasmus presented the Necklace of the Sleepless Queen to his wife and where his family was destroyed. Blood is splattered over every surface, the chairs are knocked over, and the room is in disarray. A display cupboard full of fine dishes has been knocked over and everything inside it has been shattered.

Agatha Foxlowe (see The Foxlowe Family: p84 for a more detailed description of her current state) hangs here above the dining room table in place of the chandelier, and the appearance of strangers will cause her to beg for help.

Main Entrance

The front door is unlocked, but nothing seems amiss.

Office

Foxlowe was nothing if not a workaholic, and he worked at home almost as much as he did from his London offices.

The main feature of this room is his desk. The desk contains many signed contracts and ownership deeds for both properties and shares. The shares in his companies seem to be worth about 175000sp, the house worth almost 100000sp, and various other property and holdings worth 150000sp currently. However, these are copies (Foxlowe's solicitors and business offices contain other copies), and any attempt to sell them through the proper markets (no fence will touch these) will expose the selling party as thieves. Also in the desk is a wheellock pistol, loaded, but not cocked.

The bookshelves that stand against the walls are filled with accounting ledgers, shipping manifests, and other records of that sort. Nothing current, but they contain a full history of everything that Foxlowe has been associated with going back several years. A large safe stands against the south wall (12 numbers each on 3 dials, combination 12-5-1) and contains more fungible assets: 1500cp, 1925sp, and 633gp in cash, 10 gold bars worth 1000sp each, and jewelry totaling 5000sp in value. The safe weighs almost a ton and is not easily transported.

On the floor near the south wall is a smashed clock, missing most of its inner workings and face.

Parlor

The furniture here is spattered with blood. Several broken children's toys litter the floor.

Hanging on the north wall is a portrait of a bride and groom. The plate on the frame reads:

Erasmus Sylvester Foxlowe and
Myrna Richrom Foxlowe
Married June 15, 1613

Above the portrait are two swords mounted on the wall.

Lower Level

The smell of smoke is strong in the air, and even though it has largely dissipated, the lingering smoke will still sting the eyes of anyone venturing downstairs.

Cesspit Drain

A man's bloody clothes (the cook's, see the Kitchen) have been stuffed into the hole here.

Those listening at the drain will hear skittering and scratches, as if there are a great number of rats, or perhaps bugs, somewhere down in the pipes.

Kitchen

The entire place smells of burned meat and smoke. The morning after the Thing emerged from the Necklace, the family's cook, Roger Thornborough, who lives elsewhere, but comes in to prepare the family's main meal of the day, arrived to perform his usual duties. He was killed, sliced, diced, fried, boiled, roasted, grilled, and smoked. His remains have been sitting here in various cookpots and on a spit in the fireplace for a couple days now and are indistinguishable from pork. They have not decayed though—no insect will touch them.

Pantry

The house's store of non-perishable goods is here. It is uncontaminated.

Servant's Chambers

The head groundskeeper, Samuel Longfellow, his wife Dorothy, and their newborn child Charles lived in this room. The large bed, cradle, and various possessions are consistent with this. They were simple people, without much education or ambition; just happy for Samuel to have a job and for them to now have a healthy baby. Hidden in the mattress is the family's savings: 142sp. The wife's body is here, with her child shoved back in from whence it came, resulting in both of their deaths.

Store

This is where the kitchen's supply of perishable goods is kept. It is starting to spoil.

Storage

This is where the family's oft-used supplies are kept. Bedding, extra curtains, tablecloths, rugs, and things of that sort.

Sean Foxlowe (see The Foxlowe Family: p88) is here.

Washhouse

The family's laundry was done here (and often hung out to dry just outside). An immense amount of clothing and nappies and various dirty materials is piled up here.

Cellar

All sorts of furniture and packed items belonging to past residents of the house are stored here, packed tight up to the ceiling with only the slimmest of paths leading through the junk. Only some items near the stairs and outside door belong to the Foxlowes. Near the outside door, about a dozen circular spots are free from dust; casks of something were obviously stored here until just recently.

It would take some time to search through it all. Every turn that someone (or a group) tries, roll 3d10 on the following table:

3	A rare old tome functioning as a spell book containing 1 Level 7 Magic-User spell.
4	A rare old tome functioning as a spell book containing 1 Level 6 Magic-User spell.
5	A rare old tome functioning as a spell book containing 1 Level 5 Magic-User spell.
6	A rare old tome functioning as a spell book containing 1d2 Magic-User spells of Levels 3 or 4.
7	A rare old tome functioning as a spell book containing 1d4 Magic-User spells of Levels 1 or 2.
8	Item of good value worth 2d100sp.
9	Item of value worth 1d100sp.
10	Small trinket worth 2d10sp.
11-22	Nothing of value.
23	Small trinket worth 2d10sp.
24	Item of value worth 1d100sp.
25	Item of value worth 2d100sp.
26	Book of Latin prayers, functioning as a Cleric scroll containing 1d4 Cleric spells of Levels 1 or 2.
27	Book of Latin prayers functioning as a Cleric scroll containing 1d2 Cleric spells of Levels 3 or 4.
28	Book of Latin prayers functioning as a Cleric scroll containing 1 Level 5 Cleric spell.
29	Book of Latin prayers functioning as a Cleric scroll containing 1 Level 6 Cleric spell.
30	Book of Latin prayers functioning as a Cleric scroll containing 1 Level 7 Cleric spell.

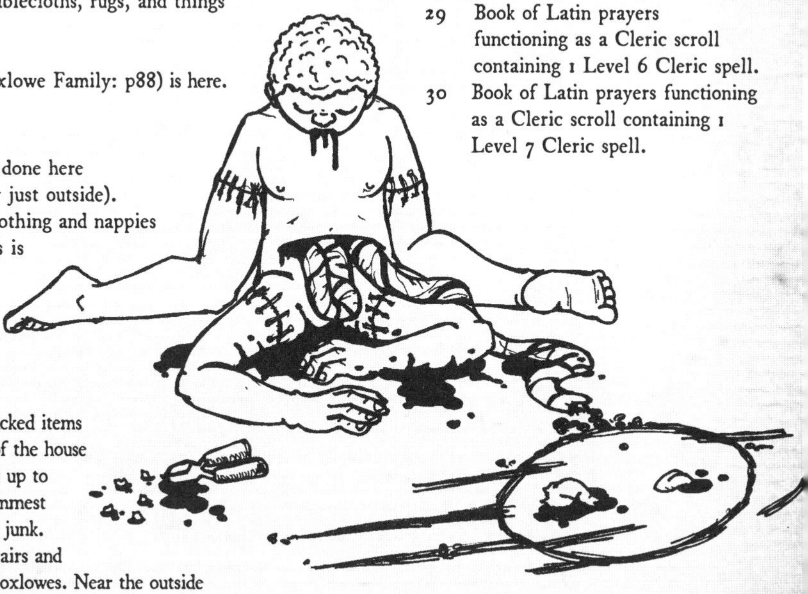

First Floor

Bedroom #1

This is used as a guestroom. It is fully furnished and prepared to receive someone if necessary, but at the present time it is undisturbed.

Eldest Son's Room

This is the room of Miles Foxlowe, first born son of the family. His room is lavishly furnished, and he has a small arsenal on the wall: A sword, shield, Swiss halberd, a musket (though no shot or powder is present), even a full suit of armor mounted on a stand in the corner. All of it is sized for a boy of about ten years of age.

Miles (see The Foxlowe Family: p88) is in his room.

Ladies' Dressing Chamber

Myrna's wardrobe, makeup, and jewelry are here. Her dresses are extravagant in themselves (worth a total of 500sp), but her great collection of jewelry (worth 8000sp total) is probably of more interest to thieves.

Master Bedroom

Mounted on the walls are two muskets. A small amount of shot and powder is kept in a bedside table.

On the mantle of the fireplace is an idol of St. McIver. In a lockbox under the bed (the key is on the dresser) are 945cp, 493sp, and 347gp. (The gold will not be here if robbers have already been to the house.)

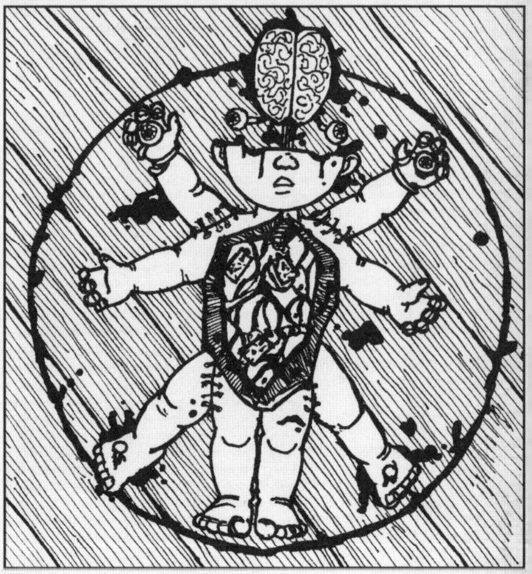

Second Floor

Daughter's Room

This is Agatha Foxlowe's room. It is decorated as one would expect for a girl spoiled rotten by her parents, lots of pink and lace and frills and ponies and storybooks. She even has a desk which has basic mathematical, religious, and history books as Nanny Newguard is strict in making sure that young Agatha keeps up with her lessons.

The room is untouched.

Grandmother's Room

This is Erasmus' mother's room, and she has lived her since her husband died twelve years ago.

The room is rather sparsely furnished, with only a rocking chair and knitting supplies to be found aside from the standard bed and wardrobe. Inside the wardrobe is a jewelry box containing pieces worth 1500sp, plus the Necklace of the Sleepless Queen which has been placed here.

Prominently displayed on the wall in an elaborate frame is a hand-crafted certificate proclaiming Penelope Fitzherbert to be a member of the Pembrooktonshire Gardening Society. Fitzherbert was her maiden name and she joined the society before she married Erasmus' father.

Penelope's balcony is full of flowers and other plants. A marble cupid statue (worth 1000sp, but very heavy) is here as well.

Nanny's Room

This is the personal chamber of Sabrina Newguard, the 21-year old nanny to the younger Foxlowe children.

Conrad Foxlowe (see The Foxlowe Family: p89) is here.

On her desk is a letter from one "Avulon," describing an exciting astronomical discovery involving alternate spheres orbiting stars or some nonsense, and a wish for Sabrina to visit when her current duties allow. Newguard has begun writing a letter, "Dearest Uncle, I am very excited to hear—" Avulon's return address is a business outside of Glasgow.

Also on the desk is Newguard's Bible, with her full name printed in the inside cover: Sabrina Calcidius Newguard.

Newguard considers herself to be something of an amateur natural philosopher, and her bookshelf contains numerous books by names such as Galileo Galilei, Copernicus, Nicholas Hill, Johannes Kepler, Tycho Brahe, and Francis Bacon.

The dresser contains her savings (233cp, 195sp, 45gp) and a jewelry box contains various items of jewelry worth 690sp.

A small telescope (worth 2500sp) sits on the balcony outside her room. If the telescope is sold, word will eventually get back to Sabrina's uncle that it is no longer in his niece's possession. The telescope is a unique piece and the market for such things is small and word gets around.

Servant's Room #1

This room belonged to the 35-year old housekeeper, Sarah Fogel. As she was not someone that Erasmus loved, she was hunted down and torn apart. Her head is mounted on the wall like a sporting trophy, her chest opened up, filled with bedding material and sewn up again (her body is unnaturally bloated as a result) and all of her fingers split up the middle.

The room is covered in gore, but is otherwise unremarkable. Her meager savings added up to 283sp, which are kept in the dresser.

Servant's Room #2

This is the two junior maids' (Tabitha Hammond and Eleanor Smittsby) living quarters. They are two young women from proper, if poor, backgrounds and have very little savings between them (about 12sp). The room is simply furnished.

If a gang of robbers has preceded the player characters to the house, three of their bodies are here. They will be dressed in maid uniforms and arranged as a display with the help of wire and beams. One is on all fours, with his belly opened and his guts spilled all over the floor, scrubbing brush in hand as if to clean up his own mess. Another is sitting up in bed, abdomen oddly distended, but otherwise intact. His gut is filled with the 347gp that he was force fed (this money will not be found in the master bedroom if this is the case). The third is sitting in the corner, large knife in hand. His legs up to his knees, including flesh and bone, have been diced, and his is posed as if he was doing it himself. The cubes of the robber's lower limbs sit in a mixing bowl placed between his legs.

Twins' Room

This is the room of Conrad and Sean Foxlowe, 1-year old twins. The room is furnished only with their cribs, a table for nappy changing, a large pot of water, and a large supply of cloth nappies. A few toys are stored in a box, but the twins usually play elsewhere.

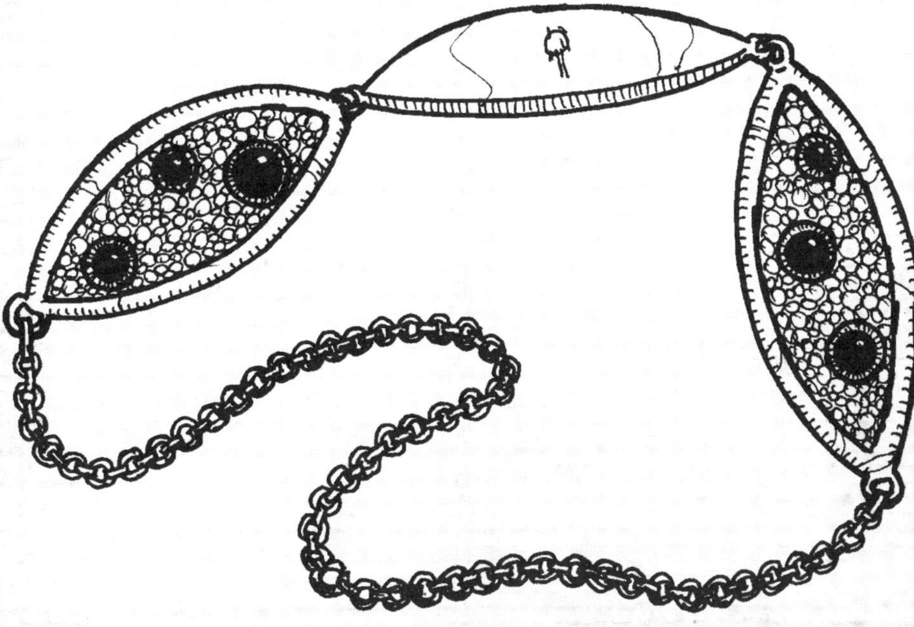

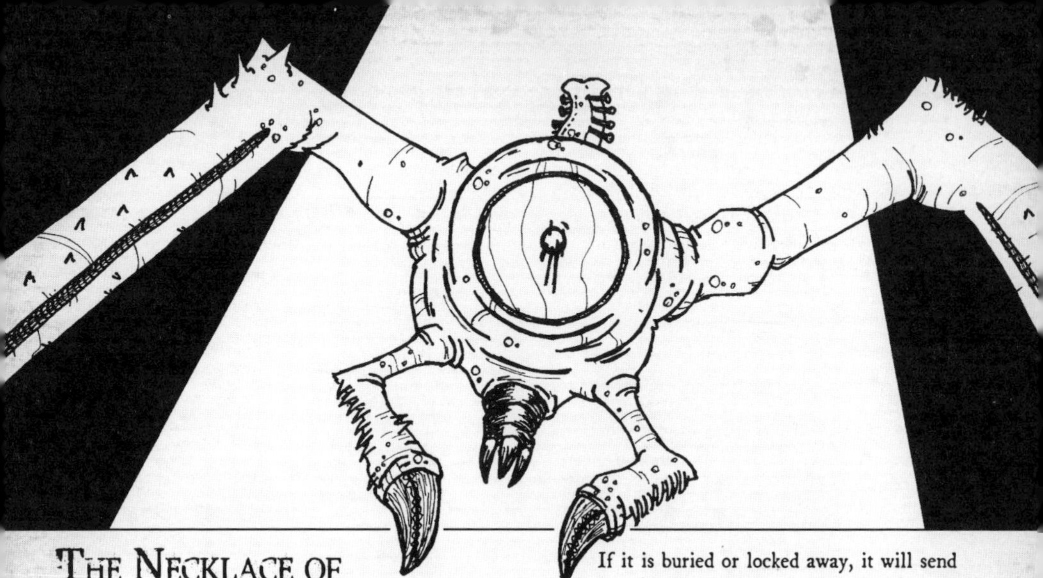

The Necklace of the Sleepless Queen

This appears to be nothing more than an incredibly valuable necklace of gold and jewels (worth 2500sp). No means magical nor mundane will detect that it is anything but that. In most circumstances, it will simply be a valuable piece of jewelry.

When given to another out of love, it will activate. The Thing in the Jewel will emerge, along with its two servant drones, and go to work. Its purpose is to destroy the giver and receiver of the gift, and all nearby that they love, in a way that leaves them alive, but in the maximum possible pain. Any who are not loved by the gift giver can be simply dispatched.

Anyone attempting to destroy the necklace will cause it to increase in value, in 500sp increments until the vandal decides it is too valuable to destroy. If the characters make it clear that they are going to destroy it regardless, the Referee should ask them one more time: "How much does this thing need to be worth in order for you not to destroy it?" It will increase to that value.

If it is destroyed anyway (and characters should not receive any experience points for treasure they destroy), the destruction will release the Thing in the Jewel and it will destroy any living thing encountered. If it succeeds, it will then find refuge in the most valuable nearby object (again, it will be undetectable) and the whole thing will start over again. If the Thing has already been defeated when the necklace is destroyed, it will move into the most valuable nearby object, hibernating 444 days before the new object takes on the properties of Necklace of the Sleepless Queen.

If it is buried or locked away, it will send telepathic impressions to passing explorers, thieves, etc. inspiring them to dig it up or steal it, and so on.

The Thing in the Jewel

Armor 16, Move 120', HD 12, 1d8 appendage attacks doing 1d8 damage each or special Polymorph Attack, Morale 12

In combat, if an opponent's Hit Points are overcome, or if it does exactly 8 points of damage with a single blow (this last condition allows the victim a saving throw versus Paralyzation if they have Hit Points remaining), the Thing can rearrange the target, making a mockery of their natural form and creating a freak of nature. This leaves the victim alive, but forever maimed; even a Cure spell will simply stabilize the current form and not return to their previous one. The Thing can also transfer this ability to another (as in this adventure with the mother-in-law) who then possesses the same ability. This is not true shape changing magic, as all the original body parts must be accounted for and it is merely rearranging (or adding to, using nearby items) what was originally there.

If defeated in combat, the Thing's physical body will die, but its essence will retreat into the Necklace of the Sleepless Queen, regenerating to full strength in 444 minutes. If the Necklace is destroyed before this regeneration is complete, it will make its home in a new jewel, as described above.

The Thing is a creature created personally by the Dead King of Duvan'Ku to destroy love in the most painful manner possible in order to bring chaos and despair to the masses.

To best accomplish this, the Thing took the two things that humans love most—family and wealth—and created the Necklace to be the perfect bait and method of transference. It had intended to trap the Dead King and his Sleepless Queen in this manner, but the Duvan'Ku were too disciplined, feeling neither love nor true greed.

The Necklace was transported from the Dead City down the Nile to Memphis, and from there transported via the Silk Road to China, not returning to the West until the time of the Black Death. It was traded around the Near East until recently when it was sold to a Dutch merchant, and then to Erasmus Foxlowe. In all this time, the Necklace has only twice been given out of love, both times by brigands who had stolen the thing.

The Thing has plans in England. The newly crowned Charles I, it has learned from Erasmus' thoughts, is soon to wed Henrietta Maria of France. This house being so close to London, if the Thing can amass a spectacular body count, the Crown will become aware of the situation, and if such a valuable necklace were to be found when the King's attention is focused, why, perhaps it could find itself becoming a wedding gift for his bride...

(The ceremony will be conducted at St. Augustine's Abbey in Canterbury. Maria's own Roman Catholic faith will prevent this from being an Anglican service, but local priest Timothy Burns will officiate, having caught Maria's favor by also being something of an artist.)

Flesh-Mover

Move 120'

The Flesh-Mover is an independent psychic drone projected by The Thing and cannot on its own be damaged. It exists to attach itself to the giver of the gift and the giver's greatest love. It climbs on the victim's back, steadies itself with its legs, burrows its head into the back of the victim's head, and rams its tail into the victim's lower back, trying to pierce through to the front.

Because it is a psychic projection it does not use the usual combat methods. When it is within attack range of its intended victim, that victim must make a saving throw versus Paralyzation to avoid the attack. If the save is unsuccessful, the drone will fully attach itself after three more rounds.

During this time, it can be grabbed and pulled off. To determine if this is successful, roll 1d20 and add the Strength scores of all helping in this effort (the victim cannot help with this), and if this is greater than or equal to the Flesh-Mover's total of 1d20+30, it is removed. This removal causes 1d4 damage to the victim if it happens in the first round, 2^d6 if it happens in the third round, or 3^d8 if in the third round. If it is successfully detached, it will simply attempt to reattach itself.

If it successfully mounts its victim, it will direct the victim's movement, but does not have sufficient skill to control its host's fine motor control so it cannot run, grasp anything, or influence speech.

A Flesh-Mover mounted on a female can attack others with the end of its tail (a stinger which strikes as a 4 Hit Dice creature and inflicts 1d6 damage, injecting poison if damaged rolled is a 5 or 6, requiring a save versus Poison to avoid death).

Flesh-Movers' tails do not exit through the front of male victims, but instead fill in their genitalia. The Flesh-Mover may then shoot a black ooze from the genitalia (aiming it where it pleases) up to 30' away. Victims in this area (a 45° arc) must save versus Breath Weapon or take 1d4 points of damage from the acidic nature of the ooze. It can shoot at a single target if it chooses, and if the target fails its save it is subject to the effects of a Web spell that lasts 1d6+4 rounds. This also inflicts 1d4 points of damage per round on the target. In mêlée combat, it can attack with its stinger, but has no ability to inject poison.

The victim is not protected from attack, and if knocked unconscious the Flesh-Mover will still control the body. If instead, the victim is killed, the Flesh-Mover will disengage and return to the Necklace, its work completed.

A mounted victim will retain his full mental faculties and all senses. He will be able to freely communicate verbally (or telepathically or using sign language) while under the Drone's control.

The Flesh-Movers will dissipate if the Thing in the Jewel is forced to retreat back into the Necklace or some other bauble, only to reappear when the Jewel is next given out of love.

The Foxlowe Family

Erasmus Sylvester Foxlowe

A very healthy man in his early 40s (certainly healthy enough to keep up with a wife nearly 20 years his junior), Erasmus will scream at anyone that he encounters, "Forget about me! Save them! Save everyone else!" He is in too much pain and mental anguish to carry on a normal conversation of course, but if anyone tries to get information out of him (while his body attempts to kill them, of course), he can only answer in one or two word exclamations. When in mêlée combat, he will whisper to his opponent, "It was the necklace, not me. The necklace!"

Erasmus is Armor 12, Movement 30', 1st level Fighter, 8hp, 1 stinger attacking as a 4HD creature doing 1d6 damage, Morale 12. He can also shoot a black ooze from his genitalia (aiming it where he pleases) up to 30' away. Victims in this area (a 45° arc) must save versus Breath Weapon or take 1d4 points of damage from the acidic nature of the ooze. It can shoot at a single target if it chooses, and if the target fails its save it is subject to the effects of a Web spell that lasts 1d6+4 rounds. This also inflicts 1d4 points of damage per round on the target.

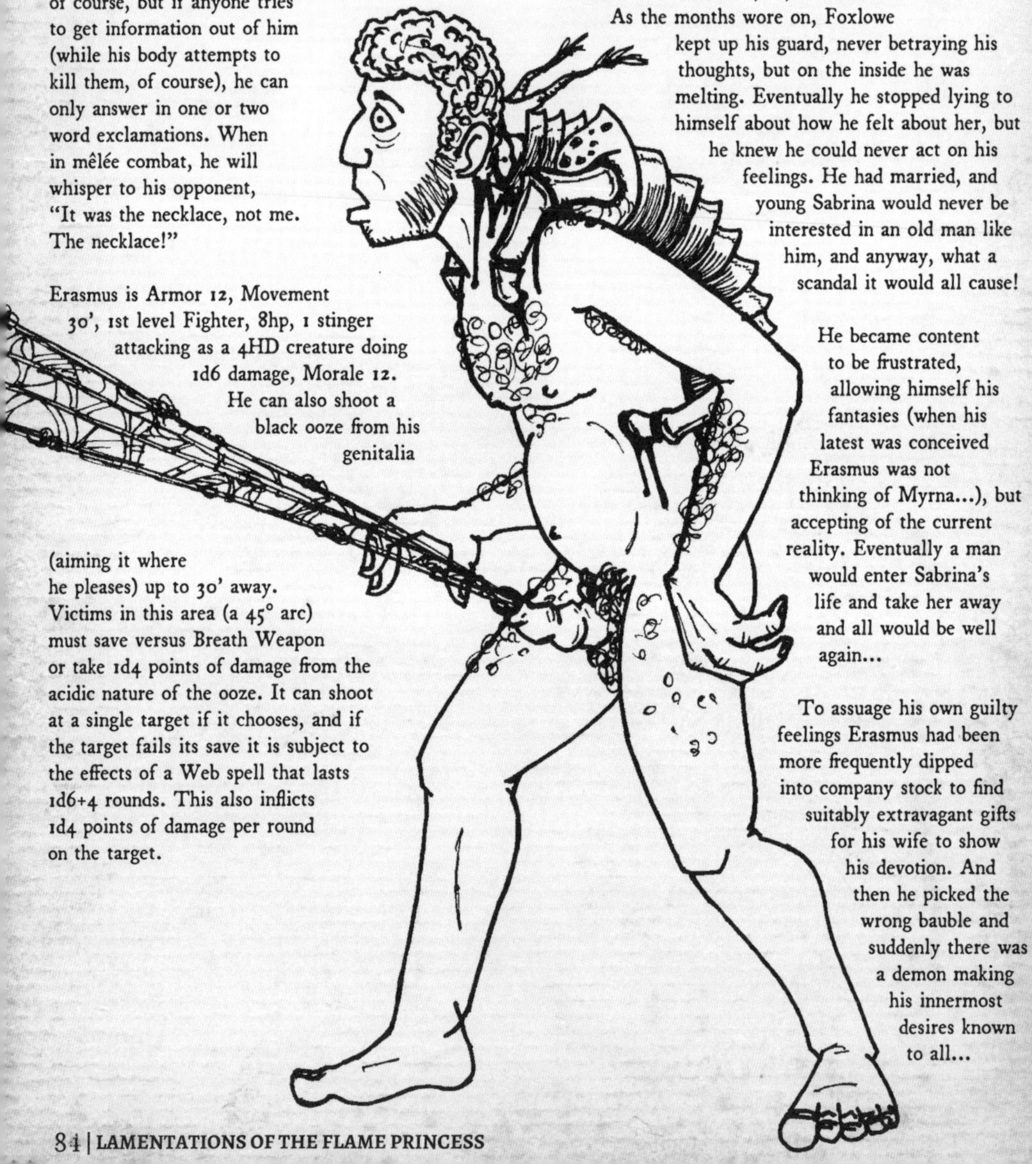

HIS STORY:

Erasmus had it all.

When Sabrina Newguard was first hired as his children's nanny, Foxlowe was not much bothered. Of course he had seen and been around attractive young women before, and it had caused him no distress. But Newguard was around, all of the time. And she was so smart. And wonderful with the children. And beautiful, so, so beautiful.

As the months wore on, Foxlowe kept up his guard, never betraying his thoughts, but on the inside he was melting. Eventually he stopped lying to himself about how he felt about her, but he knew he could never act on his feelings. He had married, and young Sabrina would never be interested in an old man like him, and anyway, what a scandal it would all cause!

He became content to be frustrated, allowing himself his fantasies (when his latest was conceived Erasmus was not thinking of Myrna...), but accepting of the current reality. Eventually a man would enter Sabrina's life and take her away and all would be well again...

To assuage his own guilty feelings Erasmus had been more frequently dipped into company stock to find suitably extravagant gifts for his wife to show his devotion. And then he picked the wrong bauble and suddenly there was a demon making his innermost desires known to all...

Myrna Richrom Foxlowe

Myrna is a wreck of a human being, as her late-term fetus gained self-awareness and miscarried itself. After dying, it rose from the dead, its mother's blood and nourishment still coursing through its veins.

The animated fetus half walks, half crawls through the house. It is still attached to Myrna by both the umbilical cord and strange fibers and cords of fibrous gore, and it pulls her by the womb. It is agony for Myrna, never mind the horror of her miscarriage coming to life and stalking the halls of her home...

The fetus is Armor 12, Movement 30', 1HD, Morale 12. It has two attacks, but is able to use only one of them per round. It can summon ropey interior bits out of Myrna and use them to restrain and strangle all enemies within 20' of itself. The victim(s) must make a saving throw versus Paralyzation to avoid being ensnared. If the save is fails and the fetus succeeds in a to-hit roll, the strand begins to strangle its target who will take 1d4 damage per round. Each such strand of gore is Armor 14 and can withstand 4hp damage from bladed weapons.

Its other attack is a psychic blast, delivering mental images of its pre-birth existence. Every mortal within 20' who is not already under some sort of magical effect becomes one with the Guf, experiencing the joy and tranquility of being in the company of those yet to be born and gaining the knowledge that the simple act of being born destroys this perfect bliss. Every miscarriage is a willful act of a soul against the will of God, raging against His Perfect Plan in order to avoid the cruelty of ever being alive. Those that exist physically are those too weak or stupid or naïve to prevent their own births. Heaven, or Nirvana, is a concept remembered from before birth, not something to be attained after death.

This knowledge, even if consciously rejected by those exposed to it, ravages the subconscious and spiritual self with very real damage:

- Everyone present must make a saving throw against their worst category. Failure means that they are shaken to their core and must permanently deduct 1d4 points from their basic attributes. Which of the character's attributes lose these points is up to the player to decide.
- Anyone wishing harm to the fetus must make a saving throw versus Magic, with failure meaning that character can never directly or indirectly, through action or inaction, allow harm to come to this miracle of creation which both exists and channels the Guf directly.
- Clerics must save versus Poison as they are so nakedly exposed to this aspect of The Plan that they already knew better than most. Success means they gain one more spell slot per day (randomly determine which level based on which levels are currently available to the character; this becomes a permanent addition), failure means one less spell per day (ditto).
- Magic-Users must save versus Magical Device whenever attempting a spell in the fetus' presence, and indeed the next five times that they cast a spell after first encountering the fetus (using scrolls also requires a save, but this does not count against the five times). Failure means the spell fizzles due to caster error and the slot is lost. These types are shown how dabbling in the Art blackens the soul, and while their training and discipline will allow them to comfortably defy all that is natural once again, it will take some time.
- Any character can choose to burn off Hit Points on a 1-to-1 basis to gain a bonus on these saving throws. This bonus lasts for one save attempt only and each new save requires a new sacrifice of points if a bonus is to be gained. Hit Points lost in this fashion can be regained as if they were normal injuries.
- Unnatural creatures (including Elves if you use them in your game) must save versus Paralyze or take 1d4 damage every round it is within sight of the fetus. These beings have no soul, therefore has never been in the Guf, and false things cannot bear to be in the presence of one that declares their falseness so loud.

While some of these effects are ongoing, the fetus can only ever trigger these effects once against any particular being.

The cord connecting Myrna and the "child" is considered to be as plate armor for purposes of damaging it, and it can withstand 10hp damage. Only cutting weapons can be used. If the cord is cut, the fetus dies instantly and Myrna dies two rounds later as blood freely flows from the cut cord that once connected her to her child.

HER STORY:

Once upon a time, Myrna worked the tables at her father's country inn. It was a boring life, but eventually a handsome young adventurer caught her eye and despite her father's vehement protests, she ran off with him. However, the adventuring life was not to her liking, especially as her beau treated her like a hireling. When selling an expedition's loot in London, she saw the successful, stable, sane, mature, single merchant who was buying their goods and she decided she had held her last torch.

Believing her father was still furious at her, she decided to hire a messenger to notify him of her death in some dungeon or other. If he blamed her ex for this, so much the better. He had gotten rather cross at being dumped so she and her new lover Erasmus had to hire some local toughs to show him that he was better off leaving town.

Since then, Myrna has been happy. She married her love, he has been successful, and now over ten years later at age 27, she has an ever-growing family. It is all that she ever wanted.

Then her husband gave her this gift which brought a demon, and it told her that she was not her husband's deepest love. The look on Erasmus' face told her it was true. As flesh tore and bent around her, she directed all of her hate to the latest of his offspring which she was carrying, and it gained unnatural life. No one but her knows that this is her doing and not that of the demon's, but it has gotten away from her now.

She is no longer carrying the child, the child now carries her. This was not supposed to happen...

All of the animate puppets of the Thing avoid Myrna and the child-thing.

PENELOPE FITZHERBERT FOXLOWE

Penelope, hardly the paragon of beauty anyway at age 74, has been transformed into a visage of pure horror. She waddles around nude, her gouged-out eyes placed where her gouged-out nipples used to be. (The nipples are simply missing.) She carries what will one day be called pinking shears in one hand, a threaded needle in the other. A Dead Sign has been carved into her belly, and lower down is worse still. In lieu of any other pockets, she is using her vagina to carry her implements of torture and transformation, including knitting needles, a cooking knife, and various knickknacks.

Penelope is fully inhabited by the Thing in the Necklace and so uses many of its stats: Armor 12, Move 90', HD 12, 1 weapon attack doing 1d8 damage each or special Polymorph Attack, Morale 12.

At the beginning of combat, each player must declare a number, 1 to 8 for their character. Different characters can pick the same number. If Penelope ever does exactly that much damage to the character during combat, in addition to the damage done she can make... alterations. Make sure that the players know that "special" things will happen to the character if the damage roll matches the number that they chose. And do not forget Penelope's little speech if there is an opportunity to give it, if they need a good idea about what this means:

"I see you, you man! Just like my son, unable to control himself. Now look what he's done! Come here, man, and I will remove the evil in you! *snip snip*"

Penelope is very creative, so will not necessarily just chop off manly bits; refer to the condition of the children for examples.

Even though Penelope has the essence of the Thing in her, giving her inflated stats (she would normally be Armor 12, Move 30', unable to fight), if she is defeated or killed, the Thing will not be affected.

HER STORY:

Penelope Fitzherbert was born to an influential family in a town in Westmorland. She was raised to impeccable standards of propriety and courtesy, and came to fully believe that only a society in which individuals think, as well as behave, properly could ever be functional or pleasant. Eventually she met Henry Foxlowe, an entrepreneurial pioneer in the nascent capitalist markets of Europe and the world.

He met her standards of attitude and conduct while she met his standards of family status and beauty. They married and shared many happy years together. Their only sorrow was that complications resulting from the birth of their son Erasmus left Penelope unable to bear more children.

Twelve years ago Henry passed away, and Penelope came to live with Erasmus and his family. She has been so happy to see her only child be so happy, so prosperous, and most importantly, so good.

Then the Thing came and her son was revealed to be an ugly, common person like all the rest.

This. Cannot. Stand...

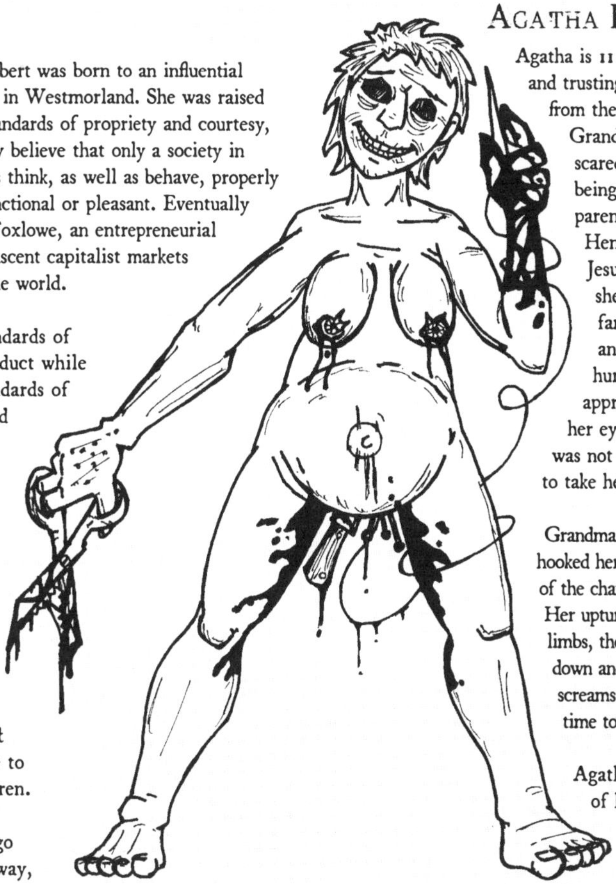

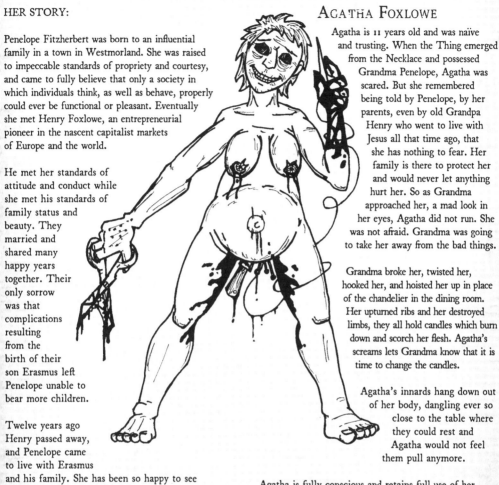

Agatha Foxlowe

Agatha is 11 years old and was naïve and trusting. When the Thing emerged from the Necklace and possessed Grandma Penelope, Agatha was scared. But she remembered being told by Penelope, by her parents, even by old Grandpa Henry who went to live with Jesus all that time ago, that she has nothing to fear. Her family is there to protect her and would never let anything hurt her. So as Grandma approached her, a mad look in her eyes, Agatha did not run. She was not afraid. Grandma was going to take her away from the bad things.

Grandma broke her, twisted her, hooked her, and hoisted her up in place of the chandelier in the dining room. Her upturned ribs and her destroyed limbs, they all hold candles which burn down and scorch her flesh. Agatha's screams lets Grandma know that it is time to change the candles.

Agatha's innards hang down out of her body, dangling ever so close to the table where they could rest and Agatha would not feel them pull anymore.

Agatha is fully conscious and retains full use of her head. She is in great pain, but the sensory overload these past days has pushed her past agony, past hallucination, and straight through to a grim lucidity. She will beg for help, beg for anyone that can help the pain stop (healing with Cure spells only make her current form the default; a surgeon would have to work on her to get her human-shaped again, but with only a 15 percent chance of Agatha surviving the procedure and never having use of her limbs again).

Agatha can tell the story of what happened. "One night after dinner, Daddy told everyone that he had a very special present for Mommy. It was a very pretty necklace! But then a big monster and two smaller monsters came out of the necklace! And the big monster told the smaller monsters to get the lovers, and they jumped on Daddy and Nanny Newguard! Then Mommy and Grandma started yelling at Daddy and the help ran away screaming and so did Miles and then the big monster hurt Grandma! Then Grandma came to get me, and now I'm here."

Miles Elroy Foxlowe

Miles is—or was until recently, to be accurate—an athletic young boy looking forward to joining the family business and traveling the world searching for lost relics. He has been studying and practicing maritime lore and knots, and is very mature for his 11 years.

Miles was butchered by his grandmother after the Thing appeared. She cut off his arms, legs, tongue, and genitals with her pinking shears. She pulled his teeth out with pliers. She then sewed the limbs onto different stumps, crooked, before stitching up any remaining wounds. Penelope then slit Miles' abdomen open, severed the colon, and used the feces she squeezed out to draw a Dead Sign sigil on the floor beside Miles. In its circle she placed his tongue and genitals.

The Dead Sign is a trap for anyone who touches Miles (indirect contact included). When contact is made with him, the feces sigil will ignite, filling the room (and possibly entire house) with a foul smoke. The boy's severed bits will also activate:

- The tongue will fly into the mouth of the person who touched him (save versus Paralyzation to avoid, the tongue returns to the circle on a successful save) and wrestle that person's tongue, forever. Speech, eating, and spell-casting will be impossible. Only spells such as Remove Curse or Dispel Magic, or slicing out that person's tongue, will stop the rogue tongue once it is inside a person's mouth.
- The genitals will transform into a worm which will squirm towards the nearest person and begin to burrow into his skin (even through clothing, boots, or armor!). A saving throw versus Paralyzation is necessary to notice this if nobody is specifically looking at the genitals. After getting inside a character, they will burst, seeding a dozen tongues (as above) which will mature and exit through the skin, each doing 1hp of damage to the host. The tongues will then seek other victims to tongue-tie.

Removing the genitals and tongue from the Dead Sign allows Miles to be handled safely.

Miles is helpless, being immobile and having effectively no Hit Points. He is unable to communicate intelligibly at all.

Healing Miles with Cure spells will fix this new form as the "default." It would take a skilled physician performing an operation to fix his limbs and intestine (only a 25 percent chance that Miles survives the procedure though), and even then the child would merely appear correct. He can never regain the use of his arms or legs (or tongue, or genitals). His bowels could be saved though.

Sean Tyler Foxlowe

Being only 1 year old (and Conrad's twin), Sean had no chance at all when the Thing appeared. Grandma Penelope quickly got hold of the child and made... alterations.

Sean's eyes have been torn out, the sockets buttoned closed. A pair of his father's eyeglasses have been placed on his head and the sides of the glasses sewn to the child's head. The corners of the child's mouth have fishhooks embedded in them and the mouth is stretched open, the hooks connected to fine line nailed to the floor. The child's chest has been torn up and a clock face has been inserted into the space (the clock still ticks and the hands move even though it is just the clock). His limbs have been torn off at the shoulders or hips, and been replaced with crude, non-working, and really not deserving of the name, "clockwork limbs."

Sean is wailing in pain, and this can be heard by anyone entering the house.

If the child is touched, the clock will begin to spin backwards at great speed, and all corpses on the grounds will rise. The clock will then stop, and the undead will converge on this point.

The list of the dead on The Bloodworth House estate before the characters arrive, and their locations are as follows:

Horse with Stanley Hobart's Head (Stables)
Sarah Fogel (Servant's Room #1)
Tabitha Hammond (Boat on the Lake)
Stanley Hobart with Horse head (Stables, Second Floor)
Chester Knowles + Horse (Stables)
Dorothy and Charles Longfellow (Lower Level Servant's Quarters)
Samuel Longfellow (Garden)
Eleanor Smittsby (Conservatory Fireplace)

Technically, Roger Thornborough will be reanimated in the kitchen, but he is in so many parts that they cannot at all move. His meat will become very poisonous however.

If a gang of robbers have hit the house before the characters arrived, one of their bodies is in the Cesspit and three are in Servants Room #2.

If the characters have slain anyone else in the house, or have lost any of their own party while here, they will rise as well.

Destroying the clock stops this, but also kills the child.

Risen Corpses: Armor 12, Movement 60', 2HD, rend and bite attack doing 1d6 damage, Morale 12. All attacks against a Risen Corpse do 1d6 damage (roll every time the creature is hit) less damage than normal because it feels nothing and its body is unimportant to it.

Conrad Wolf Foxlowe

Sean's twin brother has been added to by Grandma Penelope. His brother's severed limbs have been sewn on to Conrad's shoulders and hips and arranged in a mockery of Da Vinci's Vitruvian Man. A circle drawn in blood has even been drawn around Conrad to complete the image.

The added legs' feet have been nailed to the floor to keep him in place, and the added arms' hands have Sean's eyeballs placed in them, the optic nerves wrapped around the fingers. The top half of his own skull has been separated from the rest of the body, bisecting the eye sockets, and the brain lies on the floor, still attached to the spine, and the eyes are still attached to the brain. The chest has been opened up, the rib cage carefully removed and placed next to him on the floor. The major organs have been stuck with pins, with labels naming the organs on the end of the pins.

The glint of gold shines from between and under some of the organs. A total of 25gp has been placed inside Conrad's chest cavity. Retrieving these will kill him.

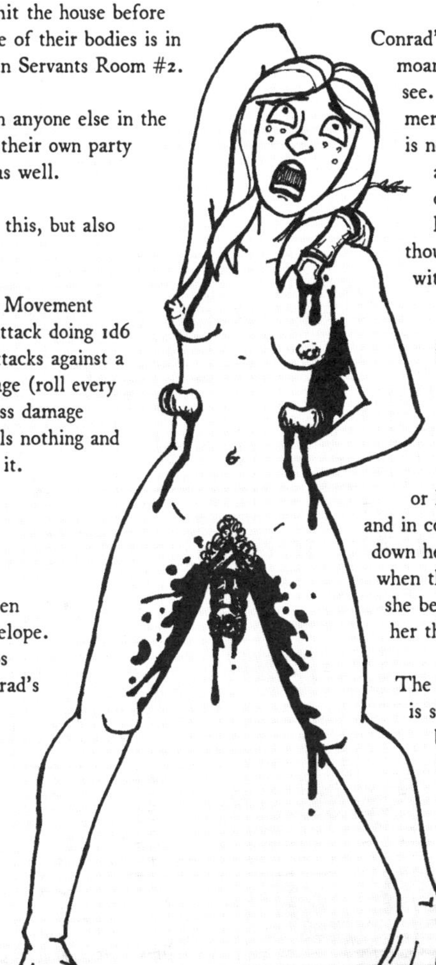

Conrad's natural limbs twitch and he moans in pain. He is conscious and can see. Using Cure spells to heal him will merely stabilize this form; a surgeon is necessary to reset his parts together, and even that has only a 50 percent chance of success. The doctor would have to be brought to the house though; Conrad cannot be moved without his dying.

Sabrina Calcidius Newguard

Sabrina staggers through the house as the Flesh-Mover dictates, but it has no control over her arms or her face. She is obviously terrified and in complete agony, tears streaming down her face, but her voice is shot as when the Thing emerged from the Necklace she began screaming and did not stop until her throat bled.

The first time an intact living person is seen, Newguard will scream for help, but from then on, will only be able to mouth the words, "Save me! Please!" The Flesh-Mover/Newguard creature will move to attack any intruders. If within mêlée range, Sabrina will be able to whisper "It's not true! I didn't touch him! I didn't do anything! My uncle can fix this!" to those in combat.

Sabrina Newguard: Armor 12, Movement 30', 0 level, 4hp, 1 stinger attacking as a 4HD creature doing 1d6 damage, injecting poison if damaged rolled is a 5 or 6, requiring a save versus Poison to avoid death, Morale 12.

HER STORY:

Newguard comes from a monied family with an academic history. She married at 17, but was unable to conceive a child with her husband, and so the marriage was annulled eighteen months later. She took up service soon after with the Foxlowes taking care of their children and has been doing that for over half a year now.

She found the Foxlowes to be most kind, and was given a large room and a balcony to continue her amateur astronomical pursuits. She never suspected that Erasmus had fallen in love with her.

Ending Notes

The adventure ends when the player characters leave the property or die. The adventure will have consequences for any survivors. Sooner or later the carnage at the estate will be discovered by those who will alert the authorities. At that point there will be a hunt for those responsible, and it becomes vital to know if anyone knows that the player characters were at that house.

All non-cash valuables from The Bloodworth House are unique and if the characters sell any of them off in London, someone is going to notice one of the pieces. It may take days or weeks, but the items will be traced back to the characters. Once this happens, they will have many enemies. It will be assumed by all parties that not only did they rob the house, but they were responsible for the unnatural activities that occurred there. Someone has to be blamed, after all. The Crown's forces will hunt them to assert their authority. Erasmus' company colleagues will be interested in making sure they are not robbed next, and they have a lot of money to pay assassins. The household members' families are powerful, and they will have a personal stake in seeing the characters punished.

It is very likely that the Necklace of the Sleepless Queen, or its replacement, will become an issue in the campaign world. If the player characters take it and keep it out of circulation, they will find an increasing number of attempts, by progressively more competent thieves, to take it. If they sell it, one day it will again activate the Thing. And if they left it in the house, it will certainly begin circulating through the upper society of London soon enough.

These problems should make the treasure gained from robbing the house, even if it was a large haul, seem quite unimportant in comparison.

Adventure Number Ten

You will die.

You will be afraid and
you will be in pain.

Everything you do in
life is but an effort
to distract yourself from
this inescapable truth.

There is only one way
to foil Fate's cruel plan
for you.

Choose the method yourself.

Make it happen.

Now.

In a Dark Wood

It is dark and the party foolishly travels in the woods. They fear not what they should and this is the cause of all that follows.

A man in a black so deep appears before them, just far enough away to be seen in silhouette, but no details are visible.

"Thou shalt suffer."

He will speak no more. If approached, he will melt into the darkness.

If attacked at range, the Black Man will have been disguised, an innocent young traveler is now in his place and will die from any missiles that strike him.

Murderers!

On a Rural Road or Trail

A young boy approaches screaming for help. "Mommy is having a baby! Something is wrong! Please help!"

The boy is from a nearby farm and will lead the party to his house. If they will not come, he will follow them and beg them, and then throw stones at them. If after a mile of harassment they do not come, he will scream, "I curse you! You are damned!" before running off.

The boy's mother is indeed in labor. Her husband and two grown sons are at market. She is maybe a month premature.

The birth will go horribly wrong. The baby will be stillborn, but the mother will bleed to death, having suffered internal injuries as well as splitting her perineum (the area between the vagina and anus).

The baby cannot be saved. The woman may be through extraordinary healing methods.

If the party did not stop to help, the father and sons will hear of it and blame the deaths of the mother and child on them. The men of the family are all former soldiers, now dangerous men with only murder on their minds.

If the party did stop to help, and the mother and child die, the father and sons will also seek revenge. In this case they are nothing more than ordinary, if burly, farmers.

If the mother is prevented from dying, the party will still be hunted by the menfolk, but superstition will draw others to their cause: obviously the powers that saved the mother were responsible for the death of the child!

Staying at an Inn Accompanied by at Least One Male NPC

During the night the NPC (henchman, hireling, associate, ally, and so on) will go to one female in the inn (perhaps an employee or another guest) and rape her and beat her brutally within an inch of her life. She will be unrecognizable because of her injuries. She will be physically and mentally disabled the rest of her days because of this.

The party will be woken up after the deed is done. The proprietor or other guests intervened before the girl was murdered. The attacker is being held, naked, erect, and covered in blood. He is catatonic.

Someone has already left to fetch the authorities. The man will hang. Because they were his associates, compensation will be demanded of the party. Harsh compensation.

The attacked has on his person the party's most important and potent item. It does not matter how well guarded it was, somehow it is in this man's possession. (The Referee should choose a vital quest MacGuffin or absolutely essential character defining item if he can.) It will not be returned and taking it back by force, stealth, or treachery will make the party just as culpable as the rapist in the eyes of all present.

If the victim is examined thoroughly enough, it will be discovered that all of the blood present is not hers. Some strange beast is in her vagina, mashed to a pulp. (It will pass unnoticed during her next period.) The attacker had recognized some minute sign of possession, and after a great struggle, defeated the terror in the only way he could think of in the heat of the moment. The girl was simply collateral damage.

When Selling a Valuable Item

This item, which should be sufficiently valuable enough to be a game-changer or one that will trigger character growth, will turn out to be worthless. And obviously so.

How could the party attempt to pass off such a fake as something of value?

This fence/merchant/etc. will also alert the authorities of the attempted fraud. Any investigation will find that the item was stolen from the collection of a very wealthy and influential individual not long before it came into the player characters' possession.

In Battle

A player character will be wounded in the next battle that the party engages in. Even if the dice do not cooperate, a wound will somehow be suffered. If multiple party members are wounded in the battle, one will be randomly designated as The One for purposes of this trigger.

The One's wounds will fester with infection. They will not heal. Any attempt to heal the wound transfers the wound from the original sufferer to the healer.

Each day the wound will get ever so slightly worse.

The effect ends when the next effect is triggered.

When Buying Supplies

All of the party's money – all of it – will turn out to be of the lowest denomination of coin (or bill) available.

Any money or valuables stored away, such as in a bank or vault or stronghold, or invested in some way, will be gone. Banks will swear that legal withdrawals were made, records of sale for property or investments will be found, servants will swear the character emptied the vault personally, etc.

Valuable non-cash items on hand will be unaffected.

Entering a Dungeon

The third keyed room entered in a "dungeon" (or any finite adventure environment, really) will have, instead of the intended description, the following:

In the center of the room is a shallow pond of water, maybe three inches deep and ten feet in diameter. The first person to look into the pool will see himself in the distance, but not as a reflection – the image of himself is different. All others will see it as a normal pool of water.

If looking at the pool while standing up, the viewer will see himself far away, running, looking over his shoulder. He is fleeing, but from what he cannot tell. The details will be fleeting; the view is too far away. It will remain so until the viewer looks at the water quite closely, his face near the surface.

The viewer will them see himself at the end of the chase. He has fallen, torn as if by a bear, his bowels empty from shock and terror. The attacker, whatever it is, is coming again. But with a broken arm, a shattered ankle, and a missing leg, there is no escape. The shadow looms – and then pain.

Onlookers will see the character's reflection in the pool grab him and pull him in, submerging him completely. He must be pulled out quickly or he will drown, but pulling him out reveals horrific injury – the same as he saw in the pool.

At that point the room will revert back to the keyed description it was supposed to have, with the party in the middle of it.

If the pool is ignored, the unseen creature from the pool will stalk a random party member in real life and it will not stop until that character is dead.

Spending the Night Outdoors

One night, far away from civilization, the player characters find that the moon does not rise. The stars do not shine. It is pitch black.

This situation persists for 96 hours. The sun will not rise and the party's world will remain in total darkness.

Civilization cannot be reached during this phenomenon. No one else exists or has ever existed.

Random encounter chances with beasts are tripled during this time. Humans or humanlike races will not be encountered, nor will their settlements or fields, or any evidence that they have ever existed be found during this time.

The Death of a Comrade

When a fellow party member dies of injury short of total disintegration, he will not remain dead for long.

The corpse will rise. It will seek to slay its former comrades, those who mock it by still living.

The corpse, no longer being alive, will be immune to all physical injury short of dismemberment. And even severed chunks of flesh will continue to pursue their prey.

In a City Center

Spontaneous combustion will produce a fire in the structure that a particular party member is in.

As the character flees, the fire will spread towards that character, as if chasing him. As if.

The flame will follow the character to the edge of the city, but no further. The fire cannot be extinguished and it will not spread to adjacent buildings except along the path that the character leads.

Once the character flees the city or dies, the blaze will then behave as if it was a mundane, though disastrous, fire.

Blessed by a Priest

The next party member who is blessed by a priest – and for our purposes, this means the subject of any rite – suffers horrendous consequences.

The character immediately breaks out into boils that soon to turn into open sores. Within a day, the character loses his ability to taste and smell, and all hair, nails, and teeth will be gone within a fortnight.

He also suffers from a terrible susceptibility to pain, as any injury suffered is a quarter more severe than it would have been, and the pain from any injury is enough to cause blindness for a period of up to two hours.

At some point up to a hundred days after the affliction strikes, it will disappear.

Climbing a Rope

A rope climbed, up or down, becomes a gateway to Nowhere.

Halfway up or down the climb, the rope will become insubstantial to the first climber only, and that climber will fall. The ground under him will open up (as will liquid) and he will fall through an abyss so hellish that it can only be imagined by one who has seen it.

Start your stopwatch. Tell the player to describe what the character sees, and tell him to make it *terrible.*

The player must describe this abyss and keep describing the horrors until at least one other real person in the room is disgusted.

Stop the watch. The number of seconds elapsed is the chance out of one hundred that the character is forever lost.

If not lost, the character merely hits the ground/water/whatever where he would have done if he had fallen normally. This will do no damage, but the character will be unconscious for up to an hour.

If the fall was already into a bottomless area, the character is automatically lost, but must still go through the process, with the stopwatch's chance determining if the abyss reaches out and grabs another character.

Having a Fortune Told

Any attempt at fortune telling, from palm reading and tarot cards to a seance or other magical divinations will reveal the following:

"Thou shalt suffer!"

And then the titles – and only the titles – of the next two to four triggers that await them.

In a Dungeon

After entering a dungeon (which, for our purposes, means any finite adventuring environment where a light source is necessary), the entrance will disappear.

This will occur during the party's first battle, discovery of valuable goods, or during their first intense search (for hidden compartments or passages, for instance).

In place of the vanished entrance there will simply be a solid wall of whatever the surrounding structure is made of, and no evidence of its existence can or will be found. If there was a passage or tunnel leading to or from the entrance, that too is filled in. Filled in as if it never existed, rather than it having collapsed.

Asking a Barkeep for Information

The barkeep will look uneasy, perhaps a bit ill after hearing the question. He will look about nervously and sweat. Then he will tremble. He will mumble, then chant in obscenities. Then he will scream:

“Your daughters whore themselves to foreign filth! Man is the excrement of God(s), and (t)He(y) seek(s) to cleanse the Earth of our filth! Being is sin! Your questions are noted by your masters and they are displeased! Die to repent! Bow down before your betters so that they may smite you so mercifully!”

He will then grab hold of the corners of his mouth and rip half of his own face off. He will then regain his senses, overwhelmed as they now are.

Romantic Interest

The next character to take a romantic – or carnal – interest in an NPC will find that the subject of that interest commits suicide the next night. The character will be explicitly named as the cause if there is opportunity to leave a note.

Note that it is the interest itself which is the trigger, not any interaction or acting on that interest.

The effect will still occur even if the interest originates before this trigger is in place.

This will keep happening to the character – or more accurately, to those individuals that the character longs for in whatever fashion – until the next effect is triggered.

Reading a Book

The next book read by a character, even if it is a book that character has read before, has all of its previous content permanently erased, which is sure to displease any character of scholarly disposition and guaranteed to infuriate those who deal in forbidden knowledge.

In its place is a very detailed biography of the character's life. Every detail of the character's life is included, even notes of what the character was thinking at the time of important events. Things no one could know are there in print for anyone and everyone to read.

The book ends with:

"...and upon learning that the book had been replaced with an impossibly detailed biography of (his/her) life, (character's name) reacted with (description of the *player's* reaction).

(The book will add new details of the character's life as it is lived, updated every time it is looked at.)

It is tragic that a life so filled with adventure ended in such a mundane way. The next time (character's name) mounted a horse, (he/she) was thrown and died instantly from a broken neck."

And so it shall be.

A Race Against Time

Something is happening somewhere. Or it will happen, or perhaps it won't happen if the party does not reach a certain place in time or perform a certain action in time.

Once the place has been reached and/or the certain action has been performed, it will be revealed that it is too late. It has always been too late.

Draw Weapons

When a member of the party next draws a weapon, it will instead be an angry venomous snake the size of the original weapon.

This will also be true for up to the next four weapons drawn by the party.

Note that carried weapons (polearms, etc.) are considered "drawn" when they are readied for combat. Missile weapons such as bows and crossbows do not transform, but their bolts and arrows do. As do any firearms that are drawn or readied.

Arriving at Port

When arriving at their intended location by sea, the party will find that it has landed impossibly far away from its destination.

The new destination will share features with the intended location. If the party intended to land on a remote island, for instance, it will still land on a remote island, just one further away. Similarly, attempting to land in a large port city will result in the party landing in a large port city in a different nation, perhaps on a different continent.

The "switch" will occur when the destination first comes into view.

Opening a Secret Door

The next secret door (and it must be a door that a person can fit through, not merely a secret compartment or some such) to be opened does not open to its normal destination, but instead to an extra-dimensional space.

Explosive decompression occurs as the atmosphere escapes into the void. One being present – party member, friend, foe, bystander – will be sucked through the portal and lost.

Then something large will move against the portal, blocking it. This thing will then shoot tendrils (with endings resembling a phallus head with a horrific alien maw) forth through the portal.

The tendrils, each as tough as a bear and as fast as a shark, can reach hundreds of feet into this world and their bite is as destructive as an axe blow. They will kill and then seed the bodies of their victims. They will only stop when a number of victims equal to those present when the door was opened are killed and seeded; it does not necessarily have to be the same creatures that were present that have to be killed.

Those killed and seeded, if not cremated, will mature at the next full moon and will each turn into another portal.

After seeding the requisite number, the entity will retreat from the portal, which will remain open to the void. The original passage will never return. However, while the door from this side is now an extradimensional portal, it is not so from the other side of the door. The door may be used normally from the other side.

Listening to or Performing Music

The sounds of the music will coagulate into a gelatinous cloud. The musician(s) will play on as if everything was normal.

The mist will slither into the exposed orifices of those present, slowly taking control of their limbs. They will dance, and dance hard. The dancers then pair off and begin to fight (any odd man out will ally with one of the combatants), each duel lasting until unconsciousness or death. Victors will then pair off to fight again.

When there are but two left standing, their demeanor will change and they will fight to the death.

The last combatant standing will then approach the musician(s) and bite off the extremities (fingers? lips?) most needed to play the current instrument.

If the musician is playing alone, he will bite off his own extremities instead.

Gambling with NPCs

The gambler (or one random member of the party if multiple members are gambling) will have a run of good luck. The next five rolls/hands/etc. will win the gambler the pot for each game.

After the last win, the gambler will be accused of cheating. If searched by NPCs, the character will indeed be found to have loaded dice/marked cards/etc.

The authorities will not be notified, but the local criminal syndicate will be. It will want far more than simple repayment to make things right.

Damaged by an Animal

The next wound delivered by an animal (including supernatural animal-like beasts) will cause a miniature duplicate of that animal to grow out of the wound. While the duplicate will never separate itself from the host character, it will attack him.

This miniature animal has one-fourth the capabilities and size of the original creature. If it is killed, another animal regrows from those wounds, this time with half the capabilities of the original, then three-fourths when that one is killed, and then the full capabilities when the previous one is killed.

Damage against the growth-animals affects the host as well. If the host is killed, but the animal is not, the animal finally separates to live its own life.

Starting a Fire

A young man, horribly injured,crawls into view of the fire. He is begging for help because he says something is after him.

If the party prepares for the attack, the man will scuttle behind them for protection. The creature will then discard its disguise of tattered human skin and attack the party from the rear.

On the Third Story

When the majority of the party next finds itself on the third story of an above-ground structure, the second floor will collapse.

Everything on the second floor is destroyed, all of its inhabitants (save perhaps for supernatural beasts) are killed as the third floor crashes down on top of the first.

All items on the third and successive stories will suffer a tremendous blow. All people in the structure will fall.

If the structure was originally four or more stories tall, the entire structure will collapse. All within suffer damage the equivalent of a heavy mace blow for every floor above them.

If the structure was narrow (a tower, for instance), the structure will fall over in a random direction. Those inside suffer falling damage in addition to the damage from collapse.

In the Capital

The plague will strike the capital city that the party is visiting.

The plague will have no single point of origin – every single place that the party stops to visit will suffer an initial breakout.

Within a day of contact with the party, people will fall ill and begin infecting others. The plague will be virulent and deadly, with a 75% fatality rate and death occurring within four days. Those that survive will recover within a week, but remain infectious for two.

The party will be immune to the effects of the plague while within the city, but will not stop spreading it until they leave.

On a Rowboat

While rowing towards its destination, the party will find itself followed in the distance by another boat.

The boat is crewed by negative men (equaling the party in number), each a living outline of darkness. Approaching these men is foolish as their negativity burns within thirty paces. Whatever they touch ceases to exist.

These anti-men will not approach within this distance, however neither do they retreat if approached.

They will fade as the party reaches its final destination, but every settlement along the way, including the point from where their journey originated, will have suffered murderous raids by, as every survivor will testify, the party.

Ordering Drinks at a Tavern

One random reveler in the party will find his drink spiked with a powerful hallucinogen. Everyone else in the tavern will appear to him to transform into demonic anti-people seemingly made of pure shadow. All will jump to attack.

Three actual anti-men, invisible to all but the hallicinator, will be part of the assault, each successful attack making its target feel as if burned by oil. The hallucinator will also be drunk within his delusion, so any attempt to fight back will cause him to strike at a random, rather than his intended, target.

Fleeing will not help, as every exit will appear to be – no, IS – a portal to the Anti-Land, which will burn mortal man if he enters or remains there. No one but the drugged character can see these portals.

The negative men, and the portals, will only disappear when there is a death of a real person in the tavern.

Attempting a Backstab or Sneak Attack

The attempt succeeds, for maximum damage, but there has been battlefield confusion and/or sinister powers interfering and the blow has actually struck an ally.

If no allies were present, one now is anyway.

Mapping a Dungeon

At the fourth intersection that the party encounters, the map will shift. Simply rotate the map to a random degree (use 45 degree increments). Whichever direction the party says that it wants to travel, determine which direction that it actually does; this becomes the new compass point for the direction it thinks it is going in.

If the dungeon is a multi-level affair, only the current level shifts, but all level connections still operate as normal. Level connections which bypass the current level still connect correctly even if they should now be passing through corridors or rooms of this level.

The exits on this level do not still connect correctly to the outside world; they actually emerge (or do not) where the rotated map indicates that they will.

All valuables on this level are only worth half what they should be.

Using Sarcasm on a NPC

The NPC so assaulted will scream and fall to his knees. Any guards or allies will take this as an attack by the party and react accordingly; non-combatants will flee.

The screaming NPC will choke as blood starts to pour from every orifice and soon the pores and eyes start leaking as well. No other NPC will approach this person now.

As the blood starts spraying, random targets will get hit. Those hit by the spray will be infected with a nine-legged cockroach-like being which will grow in a cyst and then escape in a burst, causing injury as if the victim was struck by a heavy mace. The creature has a venomous bite.

If the bleeding man is touched, he will pop, bone and tissue flying everywhere. The force of this blast will force everyone a dozen and a half yards back, doing damage as if falling the distance traveled if they hit a solid surface.

Kills an Innocent or Allows an Innocent to Die

Adventuring parties are notorious for being amoral, if not immoral. The common man pays the price.

Usually. But not this time.

If a commoner is killed without true cause ("talked back," "didn't cooperate," "tried to steal a pack or a few coins," are not true cause), every common man, woman, and child withing half a mile will also die of the same cause.

Titled nobility and those similar to the party are not affected.

Encounters a Baby

A "baby" is for our purposes here a human less than 1 year old or the equivalent thereof.

An "encounter" for our purposes here is speaking to someone looking after a baby in the immediate vicinity or simply passing within 5' of such an arrangement.

As the encounter begins both of the child's parents' eyes burst from their heads in a sick splish of goo (even if the parents are not present). They will scream and writhe, powerless. If the child has no living parents, a random party member's eyes will burst.

The baby, as this happens, will point at the nearest party member, begin speaking in tongues, in the screaming voice of both its parents. If a parent was holding the child, it will of course drop the baby, but then it will raise its broken limb to point before chanting its dread message.

Because the child points at a party member, any onlookers will associate them with the events. Rightly so.

The child speaks in a language which died out before man descended from trees. Until this child's command is obeyed, this will happen to every young child encountered by the party.

The child's command, once translated, is "Blind me!"

If the blinding is not permanent then the command has not been obeyed.

Passing Through a Gate or Other Checkpoint

City gates and border crossings often require the inspection of travelers, to fleece them for revenue, or to ensure that no contraband enters where it should not.

The next checkpoint will be stricter than is normal, with more guards checking more thoroughly. Not one person will pass freely.

When it is the party's turn, the guard dogs will become alarmed and when searched, the party will be found to be carrying human remains. These consist of a local government official's missing (adult) son, a head here, an arm there, if the party has sufficient packs in which such things could be stored, and at the very least a hand or a finger in a pouch, which will bear the quite unique ring owned by the missing man.

Male Character Drinking from a Public Well or Fountain

While drawing water, a woman dressed in rags (aged fourteen to fifty-two) that the character has never seen before will approach accompanied by a child (up to five years old). She will claim that the character is the child's father. She demands that he make an honest woman of her, or at least compensate her and allow her and the child a decent living.

She can give a full account of the night they spent together after an evening on the town. She says that she thought they fell in love, but he was gone when she woke the next day. Many witnesses saw the two together, and many were outraged to hear that the character ran off the next morning as if the girl was nothing more than a common street whore.

For every year of age over 14 that the woman is, there is a one percent chance that there was already a husband. Whether the affair ended their marriage or merely greatly strained it, is unimportant; the husband will be furious that the character dare return.

The child is, genetically, the character's and nobody is, to their knowledge, lying, the fact that the character has never seen these people before and may never have been to this area notwithstanding.

The first occurrence of a woman claiming a character to be thefather of her child satisfies this trigger and sets the stage for the next, but the character will have a different woman claiming that he fathered her child in every settlement he subsequently visits. It will only end if he marries one of the women.

Encountering a Village

The next village – defined as a non-fortified settlement of less than 500 people – encountered by the player characters, be it their destination or simply on their way, is gone.

It has been blasted from the Earth, with a crater wide enough to destroy the most remote dwellings considered to be part of the village. Beyond the crater's edge, there is no sign of damage, not even the slightest twig snapped.

In the center of the crater is a pile of bones⍰the remains of all who lived here. The bones are gnawed upon, in many cases split and the marrow sucked out.

One of the more intact skeletons seems to have written a message in the ground with its finger; the name of the most distinctively named character in the party.

Investigating Murderous Cult Activities

Whatever the cult's activities (but it must include murder or ritual sacrifice to activate this trigger), the investigation will reveal that the cult is not malevolent. Its goals, whatever any final ritual may be, whatever terrible deeds must be committed, is actually for the purpose of warding off whatever it is the cult "should" be facilitating/summoning/aiding.

The party must help this cult with its foul deeds or the authorities will stop it (or a popular uprising will stop it if it is the authorities are the cult), dooming the area/world/universe as we know it.

A Great Battle

A "great battle" is defined for our purposes here as any which involves a minimum of twenty combatants on each side.

As the battle commences, the sun (or moon and stars, as appropriate) will disappear from the sky. All will be pitch dark, with any light source unable to get close enough to illuminate any other man.

The sounds of battle will be fierce.

Lightning will strike across the sky and then all will be quiet.

If it is night, the sun will rise at its appointed time. If it is daytime, the moon will rise at its appointed time.

All of the combatants and their support personnel will be found to be dead. By their own hands. 100% casualties.

Only the party is spared.

Peering Through a Keyhole, Spyglass or Other Small Area

A man will be seen in the small space. He has the look and dress of a land far away. He will seem panicked. No one that is not looking through the aperture in question will see this man.

The man does not disappear from view when the character stops peering, however. He is inside the character's eye. The man will merely fret and pace for about a day. The character will be half-blind throughout the ordeal.

After a day the man will become violent, hitting and kicking and scratching at the inner surface of the eye. A day after that he has a plan. For a full day, the character will feel a searing pain from behind the eye into the brain. The man is spooling fibers from the optic nerve.

The next day the man will enact his escape plan: He will eat through the cornea. The character by this point will be completely incapacitated by pain. After about eight hours, the man will have made a hole big enough to fit through, so he will throw the end of the optic nerve out of the eye and rappel down the character's body to the ground and make good his escape.

On a Crowded Street

The most faithful character in the party, or at least the one with the most prominent holy symbol, passes a man wearing the same symbol.

Moments after passing, the crowd becomes deathly silent. All activity stops. They all turn in unison to the man who just passed the religious character.

"Heretic! Heretic!" they shout as they seize him. He is ripped apart with their bare hands, the intestines pulled from his gut used to string him up from a post until he is dead. The crowd continues to chant throughout this activity.

Then the crowd turns to the faithful character. "Heretic! Heretic!"

If no character wears a symbol or is particularly religious, then every person on this street seems to wear religious paraphernalia. The man who passes a character does not.

"Atheist! Atheist!" So it goes.

Eating Out

The characters' next meal will include caviar at no extra cost – very suspicious since it is a luxury item (even moreso if the characters are far from the sea).

If they inquire, the worried servants will say they received an unexpected surprise and need to get rid of it before anyone realizes they have it – making customers happy was the first thing that anyone thought of. The caviar will be available for three days.

Those eating the caviar will find themselves dreaming that night of swimming through a sea of mucus, surrounded by an infinite number of eels. They croak something which sounds familiar, but in a human tongue the character has never heard before.

Forceful investigation will reveal that the caviar is provided by the establishment owner's wife (or the owner could be a woman if it suits the area). It would seem that she is menstruating, but fish eggs are issuing forth rather than the normal flow.

Casting a Spell

The caster's fingers break as the spell is completed. This will prevent further spellcasting, or the grasping of any object, for some weeks, provided that the fingers are properly set by a physician within 24 hours. Otherwise, gangrene will set in, and a number of fingers will be beyond salvation, the rest uselessly bent.

The subject(s) of the spell, if living, suffer from the same effect. Unliving subjects of the spell will simply be destroyed.

Entering a Large City

The next city with a population greater than 5,000 that the party enters is beginning a great festival. For a full week all work is forbidden and everyone celebrates as if it is the end of the world. Sample festivities include:

All men divorce their wives on the first day in order to marry prepubescent girls (certain slavers have endeavored to make sure that there is a good supply). Men unable to find such brides are castrated in a well-attended mass ritual; their severed members shaped and dried to be used as whistles by revelers.

Divorced women whose daughters all marry in the previous ritual are beaten to death by their children using soft wood batons. The process sometimes takes hours. This, again, is done before great crowds.

Divorced women with unmarried sons – no matter the sons' ages – have the right to choose a never-married woman – no matter the woman's age – for each of her sons to marry.

Divorced women with no children are allowed – nay, required – to marry whatever visitor to the city during the festival they choose (industrious slavers have also made sure there are a number of available virile young men arriving mid-week). Those still unmarried by the last day of the week are roasted in the city square and fed to the rest of the population. Their chosen husbands have no choice in the matter; refusal will result in a mob lynching. Many women still unmarried by the end of the week often marry animals, or exhumed corpses. In case of such unusual pairings, public consummation is necessary to prove the validity of the marriage.

Looking in a Mirror When Not Alone

When a character looks in a mirror with his allies visible behind him, he will behold – as will they, with their own eyes – terrible spider creatures, one for each ally plus one extra, materialize and attack the party.

As long as the original character continues to look in the mirror, the spiders will not attack him. If he turns away from the mirror, they will all attack him. Returning his gaze to the mirror restores his invisibility to the creatures.

If any other character looks in the mirror, he will not see the spiders, but they will see him.

The spiders are as large as small bears. They resemble tarantulas, but instead of fur have small spines made of paralytic slime. Out of their backs extrude two ethereal tendrils ending in phallic heads with a toothy maw which ignores all obstacles and armor when attacking with the force of a small sword.

Approaching a Settlement the Party Knows the Name Of

Upon approach of such a settlement (village, city, castle, and so on), with the condition that the characters know the name of it before arriving so that it is likely to be important to them, they will encounter several unusual phenomena.

There will be a distinctly man-shaped cloud hanging over the settlement. As it breaks up over the course of several hours, the "breaks" will rain blood, as if from wounds, upon the settlement. The cloud will then reform, with its "body parts" out of order. It will remain that way until the next birth in the settlement, which will be as malformed as the cloud. Then the cloud will break up, "bleeding" again, reassemble in another form mocking humanity, until the next birth which will be likewise deformed, etc.

This will keep happening in this settlement until the party activates the next trigger.

Surveillance

When the party, or a member thereof, is surreptitiously watching foes, a location with people in it, or any such thing – the presence of people, or near-people, being watched is the essential element to this trigger – they will spy a line of luminescent insectoid crustaceans creeping towards the focus of their voyeurism.

The creatures will swarm over the espied-upon, their poisonous bites first turning their victims the same glowing color as themselves, and then causing their prey to melt – clothing, possessions, and all – to be slurped up through straw-like appendages by the creatures.

They will then head inside any nearby structure. They will slaughter and drink any inside, as well as melting and drinking any item that is not nailed down. This includes the party's objective, if the party does not race in and beat them to it.

Questioning a Lone Stranger

Whether interrogating a prisoner, asking a passing traveler for directions, or interviewing a witness to a strange event, as long as it is a person that the party has never met before, the party will get this answer from the one being questioned, in the speaker's own words and idiom:

"It's you! I know you! How odd, I was visited by those men dressed all in black, in broad daylight in front of everyone! You couldn't even see their faces, and their voices were more low and raspy. So scary. They told me that when you lot came around, I was to give you a message:

'Thou Shalt Suffer!'

With this the speaker will melt into an acidic sludge, except for the skull which will be intact as a number of strange worms and centipedes crawl from within.

Any inquiries will reveal that this person died some time ago, even if the same sources confirmed otherwise previous to this questioning!

Staying at an Inn

One random character is woken up by something wet – his room is filled with pink bubbles. The outline of someone screaming on the surface of the bubbles is visible momentarily before the bubbles burst. It will be obvious that the bubbles are made of blood, as every exposed surface of the room is now covered in a fine sheen of it.

The bubbles originate in the basement directly under the character's room. Any rooms between the character's room and the basement have bubbles rising through the cracks in the floor and up through the ceiling.

If the building is not supposed to have a basement, it does anyway.

The inn is now empty, but for the party.

Oozing from the floor of the basement is a creature made entirely of bubbles. Smothered in the bubbles are the other guests, employees, and party retainers – everyone that was at the inn that night aside from the party.

The bubbles contain the most traumatic memories of its victims. Eating the bubbles lets one absorb one such memory, but ingesting a number of them, such as when the creature expels an incredible amount at a foe, results in madness and suicide. The creature began as the congealed brain matter of men crushed in a secret tunnel below the inn, and its goal is to float itself to the sky to join with a cloud and then fall as rain to spread its misery across the world. Given enough blood and victims it will be able to do this.

Rifling Through a Backpack for an Item

When a character is searching through his own pack for an item, the backpack suddenly comes alive, trapping the hand rifling through it and reslinging itself on the character's back. It will then grow eight razor sharp crab-like legs and a lamprey-like head. The head will clamp onto the back of the backpack wearer's head.

The sucker-head will begin boring through the skull to eat the living brain. This will take 30 seconds. The legs will ward off any attackers, being the offensive equivalent of two swords as defending as well as a suit of stout plate.

The "living backpack" can absorb as many blows as it contains encumbering items. Each hit it takes destroys an item it contains, and half the force of any blow suffered is suffered by the wearer of the backpack.

Addressing a Crowd

The crowd barely listens to the character, seemingly uninterested. Then from somewhere within the crowd – though nobody can be seen moving their lips – someone starts shouting the character's name over and over. The crowd picks up on it, and works itself into a frenzy, and then riots.

Vandalism, looting, random assault – especially against authority figures or those better off than the mob – become the order of the day. The riot spreads as people see their chance of a better life by means of their new Glorious Leader.

The mob – now a wave of human discontent – graduates to lynching those in power, and march on the local ruler's house, overpowering the guards, beating in the brains of the ruler's family (all while chanting the character's name), and pulls the ruler into the street to present to their new leader – the character! A knife is passed. The crowd expects an execution and chants the character's name.

If the character balks, the crowd will rip him apart. If he has already fled, the crowd will rip the captive ruler apart with their hands and soon declare the character to be a Traitor to the People.

This revolution will spread, overturning the entire region's government to replace it with one that makes The Terror look well-organized and well-intentioned.

If the character executes the ruler, he is installed as the new ruler. Yet he is but a figurehead with no authority. The crowd expects him to tell them who to kill, and if he does not, they present him with new "traitors" daily – merely that day's unpopular people for whatever petty reason – and they expect him to strike the killing blow. Refusal means becoming the mob's next target.

Soon martyrs throughout the land kill in the character's name and other nations prepare for war. At this stage existing temples and churches are reconsecrated to a terrible god whose idols resemble both a toad and an anemone, and now the sacrifices can be done properly...

Sneaking Around

Attempting to move stealthily and avoid detection will awaken the silence and turn it hostile. Thoughts will go quiet. Even memory will be silenced, will all prepared spells (of all types) suffocating and becoming useless until prepared again.

Breathing and heartbeats cease as all possible source of sound is stifled.

Everyone drops.

A sharp tone – like severe tinnitus, amplified – permeates the silenced characters. Heartbeat returns. Breathing returns. But everyone is unconscious. Who- or whatever is closest to the party will discover them in this state and do with them as they will.

Wounding a Foe with a Bladed Weapon

When a foe – of any sort – is next dealt damage from a bladed weapon, a human hand will shoot from the wound, then another, and then a beautiful young girl will push open the wound and crawl out, completely nude and covered in the foulest of gore.

This will kill the wounded foe instantly.

The girl will gasp as if taking her first breath. She will beg for help and scream if she receives no succor. If battle is still ongoing then these screams will invite attack; someone must drop out of combat to comfort her.

She will fall fast in love with whomever comforts her (or if nobody bothers, the one who inflicted the wound that freed her). She is of age, and very affectionate, although she can remember nothing of her former life.

If the object of her affection reciprocates, and they find themselves getting intimate, the first penetration of the girl (by whatever appendage or tool) will see the original slain foe reach out from within and tear her/him/itself free, fully armed, armored, and healed, ready to take revenge. The girl dies.

Casting a Spell

The spell gets away from the caster and is not cast; rather, it runs into the minds of every person in view of the attempted casting, ready to cast.

The third person to cast the spell after this happens will find things have gone horribly wrong. The ground will rupture, creating a chasm 10' wide and 100' long before the caster. Anyone falling in will each cause a jet of magma to blast up from the chasm, having a one-in-twenty chance of striking a random person present.

The chasm will cause terrible damage to any surrounding structures, collapsing any structure it bisects. But the carnage does not end there.

The caster's fingers will then glow a terrible color and burst forth with millions of filaments which will seek out the nearest being and invade through every orifice. The caster can then command that invaded thing, but no longer has functional hands and must remain within 10' of the new puppet. Any injury to one also injures the other, and severing the connecting filaments kills both (cutting one or two will cause great pain).

Undertaking a Journey Lasting More than 1 Day

The characters (and all henchmen) are abducted by extra- terrestrials and implanted with probes – without knowing it.

They will arrive at their destination 1d4+2 days later than expected, which they may not notice unless they keep a strict track of days of the week or phases of the moon or similar markers. If their destination is in trackless wilderness or if the journey is a long sea voyage, they may never know that they have lost time.

A biomechanical probe, the size of an apple, has been implanted in each character's abdomen, its sensors hooked into the character's innards and recording all sensory input that the character experiences.

If a character verbally questions or hypothesizes about where the time would have gone, that character will suffer minor damage and horrible internal pains.

If a character talks about, even in oblique terms, having an implant, that character will suffer moderate damage, as if he had been clubbed.

If the character dies, the probe will burst from the chest and rocket back towards space at a 520' movement rate (incinerating the body and doing major damage to everyone within 10' of the body).

The first probed character to gain a level must make a saving throw versus Magical Device. A failure means that the probe has decided that it has accumulated enough information. Every probe will then exit their host body through the nostrils. This creates an overwhelming amount of physical and mental trauma.

The character gaining the level gains no benefits whatsoever for gaining the level. When the character gains enough experience to gain the level, he will at that time gain what he should have gained for the previous level, so he will effectively be one level behind in power for the rest of his life.

A probe exiting a character also signals to all other probes that it is time to go home. The probes will escape their host bodies (doing damage to each character equal to what the original probe's host body would have gained in Hit Points had the gained level had the usual effect).

If two characters gain a level at the same time, randomly determine who is first for purposes of the fleeing probe.

One creature in one thousand in the world will have been probed so there will be a great exodus from the planet. And possibly a great holocaust left behind if the lead character would have gained more than a couple of Hit Points...

Inflicting Violence on a NPC Unable to Harm the Player Characters

"NPC Unable to Harm the Player Characters" in this instance means anybody from innocent villagers and children to unconscious, surrendering, fleeing, or secured foes. Basically, any character (animals and non-humanoid monsters do not count) that is unarmed and not attacking and would have no reasonable chance to defeat the player characters in combat is included in this definition.

When such a character suffers violence from a player character (and attempting to attack counts, even if it misses or a spell effect is saved against, and physical intimidation or threats of violence count as well as does forcibly stealing property), that character is marked.

A marked character will encounter, at the first available opportunity, a baby (of the same race as the character) who will call the character "Dadda!" or "Mamma!" as appropriate. The baby's life force will be inextricably linked to the character.

The baby has 2hp. Any damage the child suffers is also suffered by the character. If the child dies, so does the character. If the baby is not within 10' of the character, the character takes 1hp of damage per turn until the baby is again within 10'.

The child is, however, preternaturally calm and will not randomly cry out or cause a fuss. It is possible to be stealthy with this child, although it will be cranky when hungry or if its nappy needs changing.

When the child turns 14, its life force is no longer linked to the character.

In a Dark Wood

Characters who still travel in a dark wood will find that a row of trees has been carved to look exactly like the player characters.

Destroying these trees will kill the characters who share their likeness, but each tree will have a hollow within which can be found one gold coin per ability score point the character that the tree was carved to look like, possessed.

Passing these trees by without destroying them will bring the characters to no harm, but the nearest mountain will melt, slowly flooding the surrounding area and creating a new 10 mile wide lake over the next week.

Sending a Henchman or Hireling to Do Some Dangerous Task

The follower commanded to do a dangerous task that he is in no way being properly paid to do will do it without question or hesitation. Moreover, he will come to no harm and complete his task successfully – if he was sent to check if a certain area or item was trapped, it will not be trapped, even if it is supposed to be.

However, after completing the task, this retainer will be changed. His eyes will be replaced by sparkling gemstones worth about 5,000sp apiece. He will see normally with these gemstone eyes.

From this point forward, all experience awards made to the player characters will be half normal (and other hirelings' totals also reduced by half), with the penalized half being awarded to this retainer. If zero level, first level is achieved after accumulating 2,000xp, with the retainer taking the same Class as his employer.

Player characters continue to receive halved experience awards until each and every one of them gains a level, at which point this effect ends and the gems fall out of the retainer's eyes, losing all value. This will blind the retainer.

If one of them dies before gaining a level, then by definition they cannot level up and experience will be forever halved for the rest of the group. The retainer must be alive and with gemstone eyes intact at the time each player character gains a level, or that particular gained level does not count.

This may be a problem in games that do not feature resurrection, but this is not the Referee's problem.

Deciding Who Gets to Keep a Magic Item

When the player characters are deciding who gets final ownership over a magical item, then all magical items in the characters' possession will each transfer their enchantments to a random unenchanted item in their possession. The enchantments will be activated in the same way, so a potion that has its power transferred to a shield still must be imbibed to take effect, for example.

One random currently-nonmagical item possessed by one in the group of people attempting to claim the magic item will be activated with a death curse which will slay the first person that attempts to use it.

Lighting a Torch or Lantern or Other Light Source

When a torch, lantern, or other light source is next used, all hostile forces in the illuminated area are effectively undetectable. They cannot be seen, heard, smelled, or otherwise detected. While outside of the illuminated area, these hostile forces can be heard and smelled (and seen if illuminated by some other source).

The hostile forces will not know that they are undetectable, however, and will behave normally, up to and including attacking those unable to sense them. This does not cancel the effects of this trigger, as it would with an *Invisibility* spell. The effect ends when the light goes out.

Author's Notes

This adventure is inspired by frustration and self-hatred and nightmares. It is the result of unfulfilled dreams and the dissatisfaction with those around me and the fear that tomorrow will be worse than the hell of today.

We live in a world that *hurts* just to be in and are expected to just deal with it. We don't have to. Ever. Yet most of us contine on suffering day by day until we are against our will forced to stop. Yet we pity and scorn those with the strength to end themselves early and avoid this existence that seems like nothing if not swimming against a razor blade current.

Every individual deals with this differently, and it changes over time.

I used to ritually bleed myself into a grooved dagger, exorcising mental anguish by draining it through physical pain. (It also made the dagger look cool.) Soon though, doing such things only to myself wasn't so effective. Things were messy for awhile.

These days I think *Lamentations of the Flame Princess* gives me an outlet for directing violence in an imaginary manner and enough anger is vented that way that I don't feel the need to spill any more real-life blood.

For the most part I've made such *Lamentations of the Flame Princess* offerings "fair" by letting gameplay issues mitigate my desire to burn and destroy game groups worldwide via my released materials. Not here.

Lamentations of the Flame Princess is mostly about exploring and adventuring in unpleasant situations and locales. It plays at horror, sometimes more seriously, sometimes not. But when trivializing cruelty and violence and hardship (and what is playing a horror game – or a game of epic fantasy featuring violence – if not the trivializing of horrible things?), it is sometimes necessary and valuable to remind people that they are indeed trivializing. This adventure is that reminder.

By removing the safety net and throwing "fair play" out the window, we (for you will be my accomplice as the arm that wields this hammer) can focus solely on the horror. You can watch your players squirm. You can make them suffer. Make them quit.

This adventure is not formatted as other adventures. There are no set locations or plots, just triggers that characters stumble into. They happen during other adventures. Determine an order to the triggers before play, either in the sequence presented in this book or randomly or however else you like, and then play them in that order (although A Dark Wood should always be first). Introduce each situation as the player characters meet the next listed trigger. It is essential that you only play them in the predetermined order. That is the one bit of fairness permitted in the whole affair, that a Referee is as much a slave to the next trigger as the players are.

The sequence is not magic to be dispelled, it is not a curse to be removed. Only by surviving every single trigger will the sequence stop.

Do not contact me about how this adventure played out for your group. Do not review this adventure or discuss it publicly or online or ask me for clarification about its contents (hint: nobody gets any saving throws). It is a poison that I am expelling and I never want to hear of it again.

James Edward Raggi IV

In the Skies Between Copenhagen and Birmingham

May 25, 2012

How to Use This Adventure

This book lists a series of "triggers," each of which is an activity that a player character does, or a situation or location that a player character finds himself in, which then creates some sort of effect.

"1. In a Dark Wood" must be the first trigger. All other triggers must be randomized before *Adventure Number Ten* is introduced into play, and the new order of triggers recorded and maintained.

Once a trigger is encountered, its effect happens as indicated. Once this happens, the trigger is discarded, and the next trigger becomes available to be activated.

Triggers are never activated out of order. For example, if a player character passes through a gate or other portal and "Passing through a Gate or Other Checkpoint" is not the very next trigger, it will not activate.

Triggers apply to all player characters who participated in the first "In a Dark Wood," and to all new player characters that any of those characters associate with. So if a character dies and is replaced by a new character that joins the party, they are still subject to the triggers.

Only a Total Party Kill releases new characters from the effects of *Adventure Number Ten.*

List of Triggers

- ■ 1. In a Dark Wood
- ■ 2. On a Rural Road or Trail
- ■ 3. Staying at an Inn Accompanied by at Least One Male NPC
- ■ 4. When Selling a Valuable Item
- ■ 5. In Battle
- ■ 6. When Buying Supplies
- ■ 7. Entering a Dungeon
- ■ 8. Spending the Night Outdoors
- ■ 9. The Death of a Comrade
- ■ 10. In a City Center
- ■ 11. Blessed by a Priest
- ■ 12. Climbing a Rope
- ■ 13. Having a Fortune Told
- ■ 14. In a Dungeon
- ■ 15. Asking a Barkeep for Information
- ■ 16. Romantic Interest
- ■ 17. Reading a Book
- ■ 18. A Race Against Time
- ■ 19. Draw Weapons
- ■ 20. Arriving at Port
- ■ 21. Opening a Secret Door
- ■ 22. Listening to or Performing Music
- ■ 23. Gambling with NPCs
- ■ 24. Damaged by an Animal
- ■ 25. Starting a Fire
- ■ 26. On the Third Story
- ■ 27. In the Capital
- ■ 28. On a Rowboat
- ■ 29. Ordering Drinks at a Tavern
- ■ 30. Attempting a Backstab or Sneak Attack

- ■ 31. Mapping a Dungeon
- ■ 32. Using Sarcasm on a NPC
- ■ 33. Kills an Innocent or Allows an Innocent to Die
- ■ 34. Encounters a Baby
- ■ 35. Passing Through a Gate or Other Checkpoint
- ■ 36. Male Character Drinking from a Public Well or Fountain
- ■ 37. Encountering a Village
- ■ 38. Investigating Murderous Cult Activities
- ■ 39. A Great Battle
- ■ 40. Peering Through a Keyhole, Spyglass or Other Small Area
- ■ 41. On a Crowded Street
- ■ 42. Eating Out
- ■ 43. Casting a Spell
- ■ 44. Entering a Large City
- ■ 45. Looking in a Mirror When Not Alone
- ■ 46. Approaching a Settlement the Party Knows the Name Of
- ■ 47. Surveillance
- ■ 48. Questioning a Lone Stranger
- ■ 49. Staying at an Inn
- ■ 50. Rifling Through a Backpack for an Item
- ■ 51. Addressing a Crowd
- ■ 52. Sneaking Around
- ■ 53. Wounding a Foe with a Bladed Weapon
- ■ 54. Casting a Spell
- ■ 55. Undertaking a Journey Lasting More than 1 Day
- ■ 56. Inflicting Violence on a NPC Unable to Harm the PCs
- ■ 57. In a Dark Wood
- ■ 58. Sending a Henchman or Hireling to Do Some Dangerous Task
- ■ 59. Deciding Who Gets to Keep a Magic Item
- ■ 60. Lighting a Torch or Lantern or Other Light Source